TWO OLD TESTAMENT THEOLOGIES

STUDIES IN BIBLICAL THEOLOGY

Second Series · 30

TWO OLD TESTAMENT THEOLOGIES

*A Comparative Evaluation of the Contributions
of Eichrodt and von Rad to our Understanding
of the Nature of Old Testament Theology*

D. G. SPRIGGS

SCM PRESS LTD
BLOOMSBURY STREET LONDON

334 01707 6
First published 1974
by SCM Press Ltd
56 Bloomsbury Street London
© SCM Press Ltd 1974
Printed in Great Britain by
W & J Mackay Limited
Chatham

CONTENTS

PREFACE

This book is an abridged and revised version of my Thesis *Towards an Understanding of OT Theology* which was presented to the University of Oxford in 1971. My thanks are due to all who helped me to produce that, especially the Rev. A. H. Mowvley, whose lectures first stimulated my interest in the subject and to the Rev. J. A. Baker who patiently supervised my Thesis. I am grateful too for the encouragement given by the Rev. J. S. Bowden to rewrite it for publication. James Barr provided many stimulating comments and only space prevented me taking up some of his ideas. W. Eichrodt and G. von Rad are the masters at whose feet I have learned so much, and it is my hope that this book will help its readers to a more adequate appreciation of their *Theologies*.

January 1974   D. G. SPRIGGS

SELECT BIBLIOGRAPHY

A EICHRODT

Theologie des Alten Testaments, Leipzig, I, 1933; II, 1935; III, 1939.
ET *Theology of the OT* (OTL), I (of I⁶, 1959), 1961; II (of II/III⁵,
1964), 1967.
'Hat die alttestamentliche Theologie noch selbständige Bedeutung
innerhalb der alttestamentlichen Wissenschaft?', *ZAW* 47,
1929, pp. 83ff.
'Offenbarung und Geschichte im Alten Testament', *TZ* 4, 1948,
pp. 321ff.
'Les rapports du Nouveau et de l'Ancien Testaments', *Le problème
biblique dans le protestantisme* (Les problèmes de la pensée
chrétienne 7) ed. J. Boisset, Paris 1955, pp. 105ff.
'Is Typological Exegesis an Appropriate Method?' *OTI*, pp. 224ff.
Religionsgeschichte Israels, Bern 1969.
'Prophet and Covenant: Observations on the Exegesis of Isaiah',
Proclamation and Presence, eds. J. I. Durham and J. R. Porter,
London 1970, pp. 167ff.

His major studies include:

Die Priesterschrift in der Genesis, Heidelberg 1915.
Die Quellen der Genesis von Neuem Untersucht (BZAW 31), 1916.
*Die Hoffnung des ewigens Friedens im alten Israel. Ein Beitrag zu der
Frage der israelitischen Eschatologie* (Beitr. zur Förd. christl.
Theol. 25,3), Gütersloh 1920.
Die Heilige in Israel (Die Botschaft des Alten Testaments 17,I),
Stuttgart 1960.
Der Prophet Hesekiel (ATD 22), 1966.
Der Herr der Geschichte (Die Botschaft des Alten Testaments
17,II) Stuttgart 1967.

B Von Rad

Theologie des Alten Testaments, München, I, 1957; I⁶, 1969; II, 1960; II⁵, 1968.

OT Theology, Edinburgh, I, 1962; II, 1965.

'Grundprobleme einer biblische Theologie des Alten Testament', *TLZ* 68, 1943, cols. 225ff.

'Das Grundprobleme der alttestamentlichen Theologie', *Theologie und Liturgie*, ed. L. Henning, Kassel 1952, pp. 29ff.

'Typological Interpretation of the OT', *OTI*, pp. 17ff.

'Offene Fragen im Umkreis einer Theologie des Alten Testaments', *TLZ* 88, 1963, cols. 402ff.

'Antwort auf Conzelmanns Fragen', *EvTh* 24, 1964, pp. 388ff.

'Christliche Weisheit', *EvTh* 31, 1971, pp. 150ff.

His major studies include:

Das Gottesvolk im Deuteronomium (BWANT 47), 1929.

Die Priesterschrift im Hexateuch (BWANT 65.iv), 1934.

Das formgeschichtliche Problem des Hexateuch (BWANT 78), 1938; ET 'The Form-critical Problem of the Hexateuch', *The Problem of the Hexateuch and Other Essays*, Edinburgh 1966, pp. 1ff.

Der heilige Krieg im alten Israel (AThANT 20), 1951.

Deuteronomium-Studien (FRLANT 58)², 1948; ET *Studies in Deuteronomy* (SBT 9), 1953.

Das erste Buch Mose: Genesis (ATD 2–4), 1949–53; ET of 1956 ed., *Genesis* (OTL), 1961.

Das fünfte Buch Mose: Deuteronomium (ATD 8), 1964; ET, *Deuteronomy* (OTL), 1966.

Weisheit in Israel, Neukirchen 1970; ET *Wisdom in Israel*, London 1972.

ABBREVIATIONS

ATD	Das Alte Testament Deutsch, Göttingen
AThANT	Abhandlung zur Theologie des Alten und Neuen Testaments, Zürich
BA	*The Biblical Archaeologist*, New Haven
BJRL	*Bulletin of the John Rylands Library*, Manchester
BWANT	Beiträge zur Wissenschaft vom Alten und Neuen Testament, Stuttgart
BZ	*Biblische Zeitschrift*, Freiburg i. B.
BZAW	Beihefte zur Zeitschrift für die alttestamentliche Wissenschaft, Giessen/Berlin
CBQ	*Catholic Biblical Quarterly*, Washington, D.C.
ed(s).	editor(s)
ET	English translation
EvTh	*Evangelische Theologie*, Munich
ExpT	*The Expository Times*, Edinburgh
FRLANT	Forschungen zur Religion und Literatur des Alten und Neuen Testaments, Göttingen
I(D)B	*The Interpreter's (Dictionary of the) Bible*, New York
JBL	*The Journal of Biblical Literature*, Philadelphia
JBR	*Journal of Bible and Religion*, New York
JNES	*The Journal of Near Eastern Studies*, Chicago
JSS	*The Journal of Semitic Studies*, Manchester
KuD	*Kerygma und Dogma*, Göttingen/Berlin
LQHR	*The London Quarterly and Holborn Review*, London
NT	New Testament
OT	Old Testament
OTI	*Essays on OT Interpretation*, ed. C. Westermann, London
OTL	Old Testament Library, London

SBT	Studies in Biblical Theology, London
SJT	*The Scottish Journal of Theology*, Edinburgh
ThSt	Theologische Studien, Zürich
TLZ	*Theologische Literaturzeitung*, Leipzig/Berlin
VT(S)	*Vetus Testamentum (Supplement to)*, Leiden
ZAW	*Zeitschrift für die alttestamentliche Wissenschaft*, Giessen Berlin
ZTK	*Zeitschrift für Theologie und Kirche*, Tübingen

I

INTRODUCTION

The two OT *Theologies* written by Eichrodt and von Rad are the most important contemporary works of their kind. They belong to a tradition, that is a particular way of presenting the OT's message and meaning which is especially concerned with the relation of the OT to the NT. This tradition has a long history.[1]

OT theology began life as part of the general field of biblical theology. In the seventeenth century and part of the eighteenth century this was mainly concerned with supporting the various dogmas of the different churches. The whole Bible was treated as equal in value, as long as the text could be made to support the dogma. There was no real concern with historical meaning or allowance for the development of ideas.

The first real landmark is an address given by Gabler in 1787 in which he distinguished clearly between biblical and dogmatic theology, i.e. between what the writers of the Bible meant originally and what the church or theologian taught and claimed the Bible supported. This distinction did not necessarily set biblical in opposition to dogmatic theology but it gave biblical theology freedom to develop. Within a few years, however, biblical theology was seized on by German rationalists like Ammon, Bauer and Kaiser as a stick with which to beat the orthodox. Yet, they were equally prejudiced and used the biblical material to support their own strange views. This period was followed by one in which the Bible was subjected to an Hegelian pattern of development. Whilst it is easy to scorn both of these stages, underneath the bias we can discern an attempt to allow the Bible to speak for itself, whilst fitting specific beliefs into a proper overall framework. The Hegelian period also saw the recognition of the OT as a section of biblical theology. This was, of course, a necessary consequence of Gabler's insistence on historical study, but with the Hegelian philosophy it was possible to assimilate the distinctiveness within an overall pattern.

The history of religions approach marks another era which seemed to have ended OT theology. This too, was partly a development of Hegelianism which tended to see the OT as but one expression of an idea which had other expressions in other religions. This idea became absolute in Christianity. The vast influxes of information on other historical religions which became available around the beginning of the twentieth century appeared to support this. As all the emphasis was on comparative similarities and historical development, OT theology gave way to the history of Israel's religion.

About 1920 a reaction against this historicism commenced. People like Kittel, Steuernägel, Eissfeldt and Eichrodt himself began to insist that the OT is not just another piece of historical material but is distinctive and related to our faith in a special way. These views had been maintained by a more conservative stream throughout the periods described. But the above mentioned scholars were committed to the use of all proper critical methods. So, at the time of the beginning of the neo-orthodox movement with which it is connected, began the attempt to fulfil this complicated and perhaps contradictory aim of presenting the OT's message objectively and from a Christian viewpoint. Eight major OT Theologies were produced between 1930 and 1960,[2] whilst the last twenty years have been a time of methodological reappraisal. OT theology is a self-conscious discipline and has never been more self-scrutinizing than in the last decades.[3]

Much of this contemporary discussion, whether in reviews, essays or books, implies or suggests a comparison between Eichrodt and von Rad.[4] This is because von Rad's *Theology* lacks the 'family resemblance' of the post-Eichrodtian Theologies and inevitably calls in question the validity of the old approaches. This book, therefore, intends to bring to light some of the major issues involved in the current discussion, whilst at the same time keeping in close contact with the practical difficulties of writing an OT Theology. It also serves as a critical guide to these two comprehensive works which have had such an impact on both the continental and English-speaking worlds. Inevitably, the issues of *covenant* and *Heilsgeschichte*, which are important in their own right, are also investigated.

1. Eichrodt

Eichrodt was forty-three years old when his *Theology* began to appear in 1933. He was Professor of History of Religions and the OT at Basel, where he had been since 1922. Although he has written several detailed studies, it is his *Theology of the OT* which dominates his life's work.[5] By 1933, Form Criticism was already making an impact which can be seen in his *Theology*. But it was the re-thinking of the significance of history for the divine revelation which was crucial. In 1929, Eichrodt argued (*contra* Eissfeldt) that OT theology was scientific and not confessional, even though, as 'theology', it was in some way normative and not merely descriptive.[6] He argued that all historical study involved some 'principle of selection' and 'direction of interest' as well as affinity with the material to be studied.[7] Hence, the OT theologian could treat the OT with proper historico-scientific methods but in his presentation he could show how the OT itself was moving towards and preparing for the revelation of Christ in the NT.[8] His *Theology of the OT* represents the attempt to fulfil his plan.

There he tells us that the task of an OT Theology is, 'to construct a complete picture of the OT realm of belief' (I.25). From our position of hindsight this definition, which he takes for granted, is neither self-evident nor clear. How is the 'constructed picture' related to the historical reality? Does a 'complete picture' attempt to detail every Israelite belief, or restrict itself to those beliefs recorded in and recommended by the OT, or must it show how the various beliefs fit together into a pattern? What if there is not just one but a multiplicity of 'realms of belief'? Is the importance of a belief estimated by the number who held it, its frequency in the OT, its significance within the total picture, or its value from the Christian viewpoint? These are some of the issues, raised by Eichrodt's definition, which he does not consider specifically.

Both his essay and the *Theology* claim that a chronological presentation of the historical investigation is inadequate for the task. Whilst a Theology presupposes all the necessary historical research it must go beyond an historical presentation (I.30). Use must be made of an horizontal 'cross-section' which makes possible both a 'comprehensive survey' and a 'sifting of what is essential from what is not', enabling both the 'total structure' and the 'basic principles' of Israel's religion to be exposed (I. 27). This cross-section will also present the uniqueness of Israel's religion which emerges when it is compared with her religious environment,[9] and show how the OT is related to the NT (I. 27). This 'cross-section' idea is important for Eichrodt, but it is not clear. Unless one interprets it along the lines of a sketch in a biological textbook, i.e. an ideal representation of important features, then, it is likely to include inessentials. But, on such an understanding, the cross-section merely facilitates the *presentation* and not the selection of what is, or is not, essential. Equally, it is not clear what corresponds to this 'cross-section' in the *Theology*, for, it contains many 'cross-sections' e.g., law, love, fear of God. However, Eichrodt probably has his covenant structure in mind.[10]

Certainly, Eichrodt indicates that covenant has the functions attributed to the 'cross-section'. It illuminates the 'structural unity' of the OT (I. 13), through it 'a divine reality unique in the whole history of religion' is revealed (I. 14), it enables the 'long obstructed path from the OT to the New' to be uncovered (I. 15) and without it 'Israel would not have been Israel at all' (I. 18). Although the Bible mentions many covenants, Eichrodt insists that it is the covenant of God with Israel at Sinai which is fundamental[11] – historically for the development of Israel and her religion, – theologically for evaluating and unifying the various expressions of her faith, – structurally for presenting Israel's faith to-day in a theologically significant way, whilst avoiding the schemes of dogmatics which inevitably intrude alien ideas and bar the way to understanding the OT (I. 32f.). In spite of much criticism Eichrodt has not altered his views.[12]

In order to avoid any intrusion of dogmatics, Eichrodt divides his work into three sections, *God and Israel*, dealing with the covenant relationship, covenant statutes, covenant God, instruments of the covenant and fulfilling the covenant, *God and the World*, dealing with God's self-manifestations, his cosmic powers, creation, man, maintenance of the world, the celestial world, and the underworld, and *God and Man*, dealing with man's relationship to God, piety, sin and forgiveness and immortality. Because each of these sections is a relationship with God, they have a covenant 'flavour' but in Eichrodt's thinking the covenant concerns fundamentally only God and Israel. Hence, the restriction of the covenant structure to the first part is no accident. This restriction has led to the criticism that Eichrodt has failed to exhibit the unity of the OT around covenant.[13] But, by his constant cross references to I in II, as well as by his explicit indications, he intends to suggest that although Israel thought about these other issues her thinking integrates with and develops from the sort of God she believed in on the basis of the covenant (cf. II. 10). Therefore, when Eichrodt took over this tripartite division from Procksch, he changed the order significantly by placing *God and Israel* first.

Although Eichrodt does not use covenant to structure parts II and III, some of it could have been so structured.[14] For instance, 'Sin and Forgiveness' could have come under 'Covenant Breaking and Renewal', since it is impressed upon Israel that 'these stipulations must never be broken' (I.457, cf. II.381). Cosmology could have become 'the cosmic aims of the covenant' in which Israel's relation to a perverted creation and its eschatological fulfilment could have been considered. 'The Individual and the Community in the OT God–Man relationship' could have been 'The Individual within the Covenant' where consideration could have been given to the Abrahamic and Davidic covenants, which, as we shall see, Eichrodt neglects. However, had covenant been employed consistently the tripartite division would probably have to be abandoned. Since much of *God and Man* is really God and Israelite man this would have been more accurate anyway. The present arrangement does enable Eichrodt to avoid the problem of the particularism of the OT.[15]

Even with the apparently non-dogmatic tripartite structure difficulties remain. The tripartite structure does not settle the issue of inter-testamental literature as Eichrodt believed (I.35). When he divides law into sacred and secular (I.74, cf. I.398, 407), or presents the manifestations of God as a progression of spiritualization (II.23), he is introducing his controlling concepts. He admits implicitly that the treatment of sin, punishment and forgiveness would have been different had he used Hebrew words or concepts as his base instead of his own definition of sin in terms of the contravention of an *unconditional ought* (II.380). Much of his *Theology* is a 'word-grid'. Theoretically this could be produced in four ways: with (*a*) Hebrew words, (*b*) Hebrew concepts, (c) English (German) words, (d) English (German) concepts, as the basis of the grid. To avoid Western dogmatic concepts Eichrodt should have chosen (b) or even (a) as his base. But a glance at sections such as 'The Fear of God' (II. 268–277), or 'Love for God' (II. 290–301) shows that the German concept eventually takes over. Personally, I maintain that it is useful to relate the OT's words and concepts to ours. This inevitably involves the use of terms from dogmatics and so it is essential to demarcate clearly these four approaches. In fact, if this is done, none of the bases need lead to any falsification of OT thought.

This short introduction to the method and procedure which Eichrodt adopted suggests that any evaluation of his _Theology_ must pay special attention to his use of covenant, since it not only identifies what he believes is the dominant characteristic of Israel's religion, but also organizes his _Theology_.

2. _Von Rad_

Von Rad's _Theology_ cannot be fully appreciated without some reference to his own background, previous writings and theological environment.[16] He was born in Nürnberg in 1901 and undertook university studies at Erlangen and Tübingen. In 1930 he became a _Privat dozent_ at Leipzig. From 1934–45 he was Professor at Jena, then at Göttingen, and finally, from 1949 onwards, he was at Heidelberg. Here he was very influential over a wide range of people. The scope of his influence is reflected in the great variety of types of material which he wrote.

His own contribution to OT scholarship is mainly in the field of form criticism.[17] He is often associated with the Alt-Noth school; this is quite proper as long as it is remembered that he is a member of the teaching staff, rather than a pupil! Most of his earlier writings, until 1955, were connected with the Hexateuch. Indeed, his essay on the form-critical problem of the Hexateuch, was of crucial importance for the way he developed his _Theology_.[18] In this essay he sought to explain how the present Hexateuch reached its final form. The decisive hand in this was the Yahwist who first integrated the Sinai and Settlement traditions which had previously been transmitted orally in different cultic festivals at different sanctuaries. Von Rad was not concerned to provide a detailed source analysis but to account for the growth and development of the material. Von Rad maintained that Deut. 26.5ff. was the backbone of the whole Hexateuch and that the same pattern could be traced in the Psalms and later material. He believed that this enabled him to establish two important things: first, that the different traditions were preserved and used in the cult over long periods of time, during which changes in the situation or needs of the cult community would be reflected by changes in the tradition;[19] secondly, that in spite of many additions, alterations and reapplications of the material the basic series of events which were narrated remained the same. This narrated series of events he refers to as the kerygma.[20] It is this kerygma which von Rad considers the important feature of Israel's faith, for Israel used these events to explain her position in Palestine and not some abstract theological concept. As these events are concerned with God's dealings with Israel, von Rad refers to them as the *Heilsgeschichte*.

Like most form critics, von Rad emphasizes the difficulty of obtaining historical conclusions from the biblical material. Form criticism does not deny the validity of asking historical questions but it is conscious of and concentrates on the whole history which is imbedded in the developing traditions. Often it is sceptical of reaching real historical events which gave rise to the traditions. Nevertheless, because it believes that it is essential to relate the traditions to their *Sitze im Leben,* that is, to the situations in the social/cultural/religious life of the community in which they were originally at home, form criticism believes that the traditions correspond to historical situations, even if these are not the ones mentioned in the traditions.

When von Rad published volume I of his *Theology* it immediately became a centre of controversy. This is somewhat enigmatic. Not only was the content basically a summary of his previous publications but the theory behind it had been outlined in three essays. The content of II contrasts with this because it is mainly material which had not previously been published.

By 1943 von Rad had already rejected the systematic approach of Eichrodt and maintained that as the OT is essentially a book of the history of God with men, a proper OT Theology must 'describe the correspondence between the word of God and history in its various forms'. Therefore it must be a *Heilsgeschichte* (saving history) theology.[21] He also indicated that the discrepancy between Israel's portrayal of her history and that given by modern historians would be an inescapable problem for such a Theology. As we shall see, this problem of the 'two pictures' of Israel's history proved to be the centre of the storm created by his *Theology*. In his essay on typology he tried to clarify the difference in the approach to history in Israel and to-day.[22] Israel was not concerned with any immanent causal relationship between events but with seeing significant similarities between divine events. This consuming interest was responsible for the constant re-working of the traditions which form criticism had brought to our attention. An old account of what God had done would be made applicable to a new situation in such a way that God spoke afresh to his people. Von Rad also maintained that this process was continued by the NT in its use of the OT and that this was *the* legitimate method for making the OT theologically relevant.

His *Theology* can be divided into four main parts: (1) A History of Yahwism; (2) The Theology of Israel's Historical Traditions; (3) The Prophetic Traditions; (4) The Old Testament and the New. Von Rad is unsure whether (1) belongs in the *Theology*. He writes, 'the theological part of this book is preceded by a short historical one' (I. vi), but adds that in it a 'theological picture' is given (I. vii). This ambiguity can be traced to his article of 1952.[23] There, having claimed that because the OT is basically a history book, an OT Theology must also be one, and having realized that Israel's way of doing history is different from ours, he claimed that there must be a dual presentation. Logically, however, if an OT Theology must follow the nature of the OT then there is no more room for a scientific picture of Israel's history than there is for a systematic combination of ideas (I. 121). Secondly, von Rad maintains that the historical traditions must be kept separate from the prophets (I. vii), but for this there seems no justification and, in fact, von Rad does not keep to it.[24] Thirdly, the final essay in (1), 'Sacral Office and Charisma', is not part of the historical sketch and more properly belongs in (2).

His lack of clarity is not restricted to the relationship of the parts to one another; even within the parts his procedure is confused. The historical traditions could not be presented chronologically, so he allowed the material to 'stand in those contexts in the saving history in which it was arranged by Israel'

(I. vi). Why then does 'The Revelation of the Name of Yahweh' (Ex. 3.6) follow 'The Miracle at the Red Sea' (Ex. 14)? Why does he deal with David, Saul, the Judges, in that order? If chronology is affecting the presentation, why then are the Writings presented before the Prophets, and if it is a matter of traditions why is Apocalyptic, which von Rad believes has its roots in the Wisdom traditions, dealt with in (3), The Prophetic Traditions. The structure of his *Theology* suggests considerable confusion about von Rad's method and purpose which does not help us in our understanding of the OT.

His methodological comments are equally confused.[25] He rejects any systematic presentation because the OT had its own, non-systematic way of doing theology by re-thinking and re-applying a few basic traditions to new situations (I. 121). A Theology like Eichrodt's is illegitimate because it cannot do justice to 'these credal statements which are completely tied up with history' (I. vi). Israel was not concerned to tell us about the 'world of her faith' but only about 'Yahweh's actions in history' (I. 111). In any case, 'a world of religious concepts later systematically arranged is . . . an abstraction' (I. 112). However, von Rad also suggests that we cannot exactly re-enact Israel's theology (I. 121), so we may have to abandon Israel's arrangement (I. 179), and there may even be room for some systematizing (I. 105, II. vi). In fact, von Rad deals with subjects even where Israel had not constructed the links, such as Israel's Anointed, The Prophet's Freedom and The Word of God. In practice he cannot restrict his *Theology* to 'what Israel herself testified concerning Yahweh' that is, the 'specific kerygmatic intention' (I. 105f., cf. 115f.). Subjects are presented because of their contemporary theological interest (viz. I. 192, 201, 263 etc., II. 70, 73, 223 etc.). P has no concern with theological meaning but is still dealt with (I. 232, 235), and non-theological wisdom material is expounded (I. 434ff.), whereas the OT material about man is excluded because it contains no direct references to God (I. 356).

In spite of the many anomalies, von Rad claims, 're-telling remains the most legitimate form of theological discourse on the OT' (I. 121), presumably, because that is what Israel did. But if the OT theologian's function is determined by the OT's own understanding of theology, then distilling out 'the essence of each writer and work' (II. 417) is insufficient. If the OT was concerned with 'the living word of Yahweh coming on and on to Israel for ever' (I. 112), then the theologian should apply the traditions to our day and not be content with understanding the traditions as Israel understood them. Further difficulties are that von Rad is forced to admit that not all the re-telling is theological nor is the whole OT either re-telling or history (I. 116, 114f.).

Because of this process of re-narrating, the 'kerygmatic intention' of one time may be altered. In the patriarchal sagas we are to listen only to the last voice (I. 174). But this principle is not applied generally; if it were, then Hosea should be understood in terms of the Wisdom writer who added the last verse, and the Yahwist in terms of its place in P.[26] Indeed, we should understand the OT only as it was understood at the foreclosure of the Canon or as understood by the Christian Church. This, of course, von Rad does not do, but neither does he give reasons for his arbitrary procedure.

The conclusion of the above analysis of von Rad's *Theology* must be that he had not clarified or could not clarify his methodological suggestions.

The word which von Rad uses for Israel's view of her history is *Heilsgeschichte*, saving history. In many ways it functions within his *Theology* as covenant does in Eichrodt's. The exposition of this *Heilsgeschichte* is the main purpose of his *Theology* (II. v). It is used to structure the presentation (I. vi, vii), it represents Israel's main theological achievement and indicates the unique feature of Israel's beliefs (I. 363, II. 110) and it is the unifying factor of the OT (II. 357). It also raises the question of the relation between the OT and the NT, since the divine words of promise must have a fulfilment, and the unfulfilled promises of the OT point forward to the Christ event (II. viii). Hence, our investigation of von Rad's *Theology* will concentrate on this concept.

We have now introduced ourselves to the *OT Theologies* of Eichrodt and von Rad. We shall proceed by examining covenant and *Heilsgeschichte* in their respective *Theologies* before considering some of the main divergences in their understandings of the nature and function of an OT Theology.

II

EICHRODT'S THEOLOGY: COVENANT

Our introductory survey drew special attention to the covenant for an understanding of Eichrodt's *Theology*; we shall therefore examine this in detail.

1. *The Importance of Covenant for Eichrodt's* Theology

We have already indicated (pp. 4ff.) that covenant is essential for Eichrodt's *Theology* and that he claims it was fundamental for Israel's faith. During the last twenty years there has been an explosion of both scholarly and more popular literature dealing with covenants in the OT.[1] Eichrodt's work, therefore, deals with a subject which in 1972 could be considered a 'growing point' in theology.[2] Within this book it is not possible to offer even a superficial survey of this literature, but a few comments and quotations must suffice to indicate what a central subject forms the basis of his *Theology*. Many of the epoch-making studies of the nineteen-twenties, thirties and forties were connected with this theme, such as Mowinckel's *Psalmenstudien*,[3] von Rad's 'The Form-critical Problem of the Hexateuch'[4] and Noth's 'The Laws in the Pentateuch: Their Assumptions and Meaning'.[5] An exciting, if somewhat complicated, era of biblical study has been concerned with the supposed parallels between the OT Sinaitic covenant and the Hittite Treaties. This was first brought to our attention in 1954 by Mendenhall[6] and the implications and repercussions of this are still being felt.[7] We are told that the prophets cannot be understood without reference to covenant since their primary role was that of 'messengers of Yahweh who were concerned with the covenant relationship'.[8] 'Recent interest in

Israel's worship . . . has illuminated very clearly the importance
of the covenant concept in Israel's life.'[9] Whether we are concerned with the cult, law, prophecy, monarchy, or history of
Israel,[10] or the literature[11] and theology of the OT, we cannot
avoid the issue of covenant.[12] In spite of the relatively restricted
occurence of the word *berît* so much scholarly interest suggests
that covenant is of great importance. Further, even D. J.
McCarthy, who is by no means uncritical of Eichrodt's position,
could write, 'A very successful treatment of covenant is that of
Walther Eichrodt in his *Theology*.'[13] Thus, although Eichrodt
chose his concept fifty years ago and paid little attention to treaty
texts from the ancient Near East, archaeology has focused
attention on the importance of covenants and his *Theology* still
retains great relevance because of its basic subject. As most of this
interest came to the fore after Eichrodt had produced his *Theology*,
we cannot accuse him of jumping on to the current band wagon
of scholarship, nor can we explain his choice in these terms.

It is not hard to explain the value of covenant as a concept for
organizing a Theology, once it is understood as it was by
Eichrodt. He believed that covenant provided the key both to the
unity and the uniqueness of Israel's faith. Hence, it was an ideal
concept for making the relation of the OT to the NT clear and
this was a third of Eichrodt's major concerns.[14] Although he does
not specify his presuppositions, it seems probable that he believes
that if you can show that the features of Israel's religion which
are unique, and which therefore explain her uniqueness, are also
the ones which dominate her religion, as long as she remains true
to herself, then you have evidence for the revelational value of this
religion. Further, if, as Eichrodt believes, the type of God which
these unique features imply corresponds to the type of God
revealed in the NT, then the revelational value is confirmed. All
this Eichrodt believes to be true for Israel's covenant. As he
understands it, this concept emphasizes that God relates to man,
that the field of revelation and communion is history, i.e. human
experience, and that God's act comes first, i.e. the relationship is
one of grace to which human response is necessary, so that law
finds its proper place within the context of grace.[15] Thus, religion
is essentially concerned with the proper response to God's saving
acts and God is concerned with establishing fellowship with man
on acceptable terms. This process takes place through the

particular but potentially includes all (I. 36–45 etc.). This, needless to say, corresponds to Eichrodt's understanding of the Christian faith. So covenant is both structurally and conceptually useful to his *Theology*.

But we still have to answer the question as to why he thinks that covenant is both the dominating centre and the defining characteristic of Israel's religion. The short answer is that this is what he believes the OT, examined by the historico-critical methodology, reveals. A more satisfactory account demands that we first try and specify more precisely what it is which he has made the centre of his *Theology*. We know it is covenant, but what does Eichrodt understand by this?[16]

2. *The Meaning of Covenant in Eichrodt's* Theology

(*a*) Sometimes covenant is nothing more than a cipher for the Hebrew *berīt*, i.e. the normal translation of this Hebrew word. Yet it is not the word itself to which Eichrodt gives such importance. This is, first, because he is only interested in the divine-human covenant. More importantly, on several occasions he states that the occurrence of the word is unimportant: 'The decisive consideration on this point is neither the presence nor absence of the actual term *berīt*' (I. 13f., 17f., cf.I. 36, 37, 52 etc.). We shall see that this position, reasonable as it may be, involves him in a problem of which he is not aware.

(*b*) The second possibility is that it is the concept indicated by *berīt*. This obviously brings us nearer to Eichrodt's position. After all, he begins his *Theology* with the meaning and history of the covenant concept (I. 36ff.). He summarizes the change of meaning thus:

The term has to cover two lines of thought along which the meaning has developed. The first runs from 'covenant' through 'covenant relationship', 'covenant precept' and 'legal system' to 'religion', 'cultus' and 'covenant people'; the other from 'covenant' through the divine act of 'establishment', 'the relationship of grace' and 'revelation' to the 'order of redemption', 'the decree of salvation' and the final 'consumation of all things' (I. 66).[17]

In spite of his criticisms of some developments, especially in the post-exilic period (I. 63ff.), he feels committed to the concept as he outlines it, for, although he sees 'two divergent understandings of the covenant . . . in opposition to one another', he claims we should be committed to it all (I. 66). Nevertheless, although there is some justification for the criticism that he 'forces the OT concept into a single form, when it had many, and does not do justice to the complex history of the idea in the OT',[18] it seems to me essentially inappropriate, not only because he does recognize a variety of 'forms'[19] and a variety of ideas (cf. I. 36ff.) but also because it is not the concept as such which he has made the centre of his *Theology*. It is for this reason that he can be critical of certain developments and emphases which the concept received during its history.

(c) We come much closer to Eichrodt's position once we recognize that it is not the concept in general but what Eichrodt decides is its primary referent, namely the covenant at Sinai, which is central. Clearly, it is this, as Eichrodt understands it through his evaluation of the OT material, which guides and dominates his understanding of covenant (cf. I. 36–44). The Sinai covenant puts Israel into a special relation with God, which is dependent on God's prior redemptive activity of the Exodus. This enables him to emphasize that history is the basic field of revelation and not speculation (I. 37, 41). This relationship includes an obligatory response of the people expressed in terms of obedience to the covenant laws in their daily lives. As this law expresses the divine will for Israel, she is given fairly precise knowledge of God and so is freed from fear of a capricious deity. The covenant makes its members aware of their unique position, so all those within the covenant feel a special bond of attachment to each other (I. 39) which results in national consciousness; thus the nation is dependent on God's purpose and not *vice versa* (I. 41f.). As God initiates the covenant he is free to dissolve it and should not be considered to be bound to Israel by the nature of things: he is the free, personal Lord (I. 44).[20]

Whilst Eichrodt gives this account of the Sinai covenant under the heading 'The Meaning of the Covenant Concept', it is clearly the referent and not just the concept which is important to Eichrodt because he emphasizes that the covenant was a real happening, once for all (I. 43), based on the experience of the Exodus (I. 38), and it was this which was the *historical* cause of Israel's existence. At this point, historical causation and revelation intersect. Even so, we have still not quite reached Eichrodt's position.

(*d*) For Eichrodt, the Sinai covenant is only an interpretation (although Eichrodt believes a resonably accurate and comprehensive interpretation) of the relationship of God with Israel. 'Moses, taking over a concept of long standing in secular life, based the worship of Yahweh on a covenant agreement' (I. 37). Hence, covenant is a 'definitive *expression*' (I. 36), a '*code-word* . . . for the deepest layer of the foundation of Israel's faith' (I. 18), a 'convenient *symbol* . . . an *epitome* of the dealings of God in history . . . the *characteristic description* of a living process' (I. 14), it '*enshrines* Israel's . . . sense of a unique relationship with God' (I. 17) etc. It is this reality, to which covenant points, which Eichrodt claims to be the centre of Israel's faith and of his *Theology*, what he calls 'the spiritual premises of a covenant relationship with God' (I. 36f.). Eichrodt does not accept that the Sinai covenant is ultimate because he recognizes that it had deficiencies (I. 59, 68), it was liable to nationalistic misinterpretations (I. 45ff.), legalistic distortions (I. 52) and a one-sided cultic emphasis (I. 46). But Eichrodt develops his *Theology* around covenant because it was in the Sinai covenant that the 'process' was initiated:

The redemption from Egypt received its *definitive interpretation* at the covenant-making on Sinai – and thus became the foundation and the orientation of all the mutual relations of Yahweh and his people (I. 292).

It is important to realize that Eichrodt is not committed to the position that all Israel's theology was consciously covenantal. He uses covenant to 'illuminate . . . the message of the OT' (I. 13, cf. I. 17, II. 10). He recognizes that such thinking could be 'implicit' (I. 14), so he is not making historical claims about the thought processes of Israelites but claiming that covenant is useful for presenting the presuppositions of their patterns of thought to twentieth-century man. He believes that this pattern corresponds to the relationship which God actually had with Israel. Although Eichrodt insists on the historicity of the Sinaitic covenant, this might be unimportant, for the conceptual patterns, deduced from the traditions, might still be illuminating.[21]

There are two other points, connected with the meaning of covenant which we can now consider. The first concerns the translation of *berît* by covenant.[22] Eichrodt admits that this is inadequate but accepts that it is roughly correct, certainly more so than *diathēkē* (I. 66). Since Eichrodt wrote his *Theology*, there have been various attempts to invalidate this translation. A. Jepsen argued that it referred to the act which produces a relationship and not to the relationship established,[23] G. Fohrer that it meant 'obligation' or 'promise',[24] and E. Kutsch only 'obligation'.[25] But as McCarthy correctly insists, 'An obligation is *to* someone or *between* parties, that is, it necessarily involves a relationship.'[26] In other words, these attempts have not succeeded in disproving that *bᵉrît* is a word from a relational conceptual field, and this is more than sufficient for Eichrodt's purposes,[27] since it is not the word itself but the reality for which the word is a symbol which is important.

The second point arises just because Eichrodt does not restrict his use of covenant to the occurrence of the word *bᵉrît*. Now, although there will always be doubt as to whether or not any particular situation could be described by *bᵉrît*, because the material we have available for defining the meaning of the word is restricted and the meaning the word had at one time could change sufficiently to make it inappropriate to call the situation referred to by *bᵉrît* at one time by that word at a later time, it does not seem possible to insist that we talk of a *bᵉrît*/covenant only when the Hebrew word is present. Other scholars are quite prepared to speak of covenants when the term is lacking.[28] McCarthy points out that initially there was no specific term for the treaties,[25] and Mendenhall claims that 'there are numerous references to covenants and covenant relationships where the term does not occur'.[30] But, if we are not prepared to limit covenants to the occurrence of *bᵉrît*, then the reality could be present outside of Israel. Thus, even if Baltzer is correct to claim that the use of the covenant-treaty to express a relationship with God is unknown outside of Israel,[31] once it is recognized that the people involved in such a treaty could be called 'brothers' or 'father and sons',[32] it becomes impossible to draw a clear distinction between a covenant and a family or natural relationship with the deity. Therefore, it becomes difficult for Eichrodt to insist that Israel's conception of her relationship with God was unique because it was covenantal rather than naturalistic, as in Canaan. Further, Eichrodt seems to assume that because her *conception* of the relationship was unique, the relationship itself was necessarily unique (I. 13, 17), so this also becomes problematic. On the other hand, this breakdown of the hard distinction between family and covenant relations makes the references to the former by the prophets more understandable.[33]

Summary

For Eichrodt covenant is a cipher for the word *bᵉrît*, the basic meaning of the concept, fundamentally the Sinaitic covenant together with all he deduces about that, but essentially it is the code-word for the real relationship of God with Israel. It is in this sense that he claims 'covenant' dominates the OT and this is what is central in his *Theology*. Inevitably this means that his central concept is somewhat removed from the OT's use of *bᵉrît*, though not unconnected. This idealization makes it difficult to test out Eichrodt's claims. If however, we ask why he calls God's relation with and revelation to Israel a 'covenant', then he can make a twofold reply: first, he believes that it was a covenant which initiated this process; secondly, Israel herself often used *bᵉrît* to refer to it. But, in choosing covenant he chose a term which not only indicated what Israel's faith was like but also enabled him to communicate her understanding to twentieth-century man and relate her faith to that of the NT.

In the following pages we shall consider the problem of the date and nature of the Sinaitic covenant and then the importance of other divine covenants for Israel's faith and Eichrodt's *Theology*.

3. *How Early was the Sinaitic Covenant?*

Eichrodt is committed to the belief that Moses initiated a covenant relation between Yahweh and Israel on Mount Sinai, which correctly expressed the relationship God was seeking with Israel on the basis of the Exodus experiences. He was well aware that his position could be 'sharply contested' (I. 36 and n. 1) and although new material and ways of approaching the subject have emerged, this position is still one which provokes intense discussion.

Eichrodt's exposition apparently has the advantage of following the OT itself. Nevertheless his account does not proceed by expounding the biblical traditions relevant to it, but by a process of reflection on the events as he understands them on the basis of the OT (cf. I. 36–45). At the same time, he definitely departs from the OT's presentation when he virtually ignores the patriarchal covenant – a point which we will examine later.[34]

Eichrodt's insistence on the Mosaic origin of the covenant is closely tied up with his view of the nature of Israel's religion as a 'founder religion' (I. 84, cf. I. 289) and the basic reliability of the Sinaitic narratives. How much we can reasonably say about the historical Moses is still disputed[35] and it is likely to remain so. The same is true for the importance of a 'founder' for a religion of revelation.[36] Clearly, Eichrodt has not modified substantially his original position.[37] But although he takes a dogmatic stance on this issue, he does try to indicate the relevance of his *Theology* for those who do not completely follow him.[38] After surveying this issue we shall make further suggestions.

The question of the 'historical Moses' is but one example of the inevitable dependence of any OT Theology on Israel's history. As this issue cannot be avoided it seems sensible that a Theology indicate the view of Israel's history on which it depends, either by including a sketch, or by referring to a current *History of Israel* which is similar to the one the Theology presupposes.[39]

In trying to establish the date of the concept of a Sinaitic covenant, the book of Deuteronomy provides a useful point of departure. Most scholars agree that it had reached something like its present form by the end of the seventh century BC[40] and that it envisages a type of covenant similar to that depicted by Eichrodt.[41] Most go further and recognize that both in form and terminology it reflects the political treaties:

There can be no doubt that Deut. does show some kind of relationship to the literary forms of the treaties. It has the same sequence . . . Moreover, certain elements in the so called framework to Deut., chapters 4 and 29–30, show a similarity to this structure.[42]

Here, however, the agreement ends. Some maintain that Deuteronomy developed the political analogy in the religious sphere because of the impact of Assyrian treaties in Israel's field of knowledge at this time.[43] Certainly, there are similarities with these first-millennium treaties such as the stress on the written guarantee, the emphasis on the curses[44] and even the order in which the curses are listed.[45] Yet, it is difficult to accept that this alone is a sufficient explanation. To start with, there is the problem of explaining why Israel should use the tool of her enemy to account for and explain her relationship with God, especially if this view were novel. Secondly, Deuteronomy is far more concerned with the *history* of God's relationship with Israel than seems to be the case for Assyrian treaties. The influence of these treaties is more easily acceptable if it is understood as a modification of a previous covenant concept rather than an innovation.[46]

A second approach recognizes that Deuteronomy contains much older traditions which also reflect a covenant conception of Israel's relationship. This links Deut. 27 with Josh. 24 and relates both to Shechem.[47] Usually these traditions are felt to reflect a ceremony rather than a specific historical event, although Josh. 24 may also reflect the occasion when tribes which had not shared in the Sinai experience were integrated into the tribal league based on the worship of Yahweh.[48] This league, normally known as the amphictyony, has been a keystone in the arguments of those who accept the importance of covenant for Israel.[49] In Eichrodt's case, it enables him to avoid the problem of assessing how important and influential the belief in a divine covenant was for the actual members of Israel, since he understands Israel, on the basis of the amphictyony, as a theological category, that is, the human partner of the covenant.[50] In the last decade the viability of this amphictyonic conception has been challenged.[51] Nevertheless, even if the term has outlived its usefulness, it served, in Noth's hands, to draw attention to a tendency within Israel which cannot be overlooked. The unity of the tribes, such as it was, cannot be ignored, for they preserved their self-identity with a tenacity which is unusual in emergent nations which are surrounded by another and stronger culture.[52] This unity was connected with their allegiance to Yahweh. Thus it seems necessary to push the idea of a Sinaitic covenant way back into the period of the settlement of the tribes in Palestine.

A second critical issue for the dating and importance of the Sinaitic covenant concerns the lack of references in the early writing prophets.[53] It is well known that there are only two references to a divine *bᵉrit*. Even so, there is much to suggest that the prophets not only understood Israel's relationship along these lines but were also influenced in their language and imagery by political treaties.[54] The case for the former point is clearly summarized and presented by R. E. Clements, so there is no need to repeat it here. He believes that under the varieties of prophetic utterance there is a unifying tendency, 'found in an overall concern with the covenant as the basis and explanation of Israel's existence'.[55] Indeed, it is their attitude which explains why the prophetic writings were given canonical status. The dependence of the prophets on the political treaties has been suggested because of the *rib*-pattern that is, the lawsuit in which Israel is accused before Yahweh for breach of trust, the pattern of weal and woe, and the threats which the prophets proclaim against Israel, which seem to be similar in type and content to those used in the treaties.[56] Although it may be difficult to establish that these features can *only* be explained by assuming they were dependent on political treaties,[57] the concepts implied by these treaties illuminate their message, and the assumption that they believed Israel was in a covenant relationship with Yahweh makes the use of such features understandable. However, it is important to realize that even if their dependence on political treaties is established this does not prove their dependence on any concept of a Sinaitic covenant and it is this which is Eichrodt's concern.[58] Equally, to deny this dependence on political treaties does not entail the rejection of their dependence on the Sinaitic covenant; McCarthy, whilst being sceptical of the political dependence, sees the prophetic activity as the 'application of the covenant traditions to new circumstances'.[59] Covenant concepts and political treaties are not synonymous, and Eichrodt's original position did not depend upon the political parallels, even if many, including myself, consider they strengthen his case.

The evaluation of the prophetic dependence on the Sinaitic traditions of a covenant involves asking whether the prophets thought of Israel's relationship to Yahweh in a similar way and whether they used the Exodus/Sinai traditions.[60] But, even if all this is granted, how is the absence of the term *berit* to be explained? Eichrodt was concerned with this, all the more because it is those prophets who use the analogy of personal relations who neglect the concept of *berit* (I. 68 etc.). However, these personal relations, such as Father/son, Foster-parent/child, Ruler/people, Shepherd/flock, all have legal implications and obligations. Indeed, in Ezek. 16.8 betrothal is explicitly described as a 'covenant' (cf. Mal. 2.14 and I. 42 n. 3, 251). When we recall that the treaties make use of such terms to describe the members of the treaty it becomes clear that whilst there may be a different nuance, these concepts are not to be opposed to covenant concepts.

Something like Eichrodt's account of the prophets seems reasonable:

These reforming spirits have set themselves to oppose every instance of dead externalism in religious practice and mechanical routine in religious thought (I. 51).

A further argument suggests that the prophets were essentially functionaries within the covenant festival.[61] Although this view has not been widely accepted, it introduces us to the next issue of debate – whether there was a covenant festival in Jerusalem and prior to that at the tribal centres such as Gilgal, Bethel, Shechem and Shilo.[62] The evidence for some form of covenant celebration is widespread and generally accepted, although, as is customary, scholars vary over its reconstruction. Even though Eichrodt made little reference to this possibility (I. 123 is an addition to the 1933 edition), the existence of such a festival is almost essential to his position. Its importance lies in the fact that it makes it conceivable how and why the traditions and concepts associated with the Sinaitic covenant were so influential and dominant. It is also an important part of the case of those who maintain that the biblical Sinaitic traditions are best explained on the assumption that they were originally dependent on the Hittite treaties.

This argument, first proposed by G. E. Mendenhall,[63] depends on being able to distinguish the form of the Hittite vassal treaties both from other types of Hittite treaties (e.g. parity treaties) and from other Mesopotamian treaties of earlier and later dates. Equally, it is necessary to show that Israel's traditions contain those features which are peculiar to the Hittite vassal treaties. The whole issue is one of immense complexity, partly because of the fragmentary nature of many of the extant treaties and certainly of our total archaeological picture of their extent, function and relationship to other politico-social forms, and partly because of the problematic nature of the biblical material, of which Ex. 19–24, 34 is primary. The problems here include not only the source analysis and tradition history of the material but also the fact that the material is now in narrative and not treaty form. It is also acknowledged that if such a political treaty form were used of the relationship between Yahweh and Israel then, inevitably, certain features such as the appeal to deities as witnesses, would have to be changed. What appeared to be a simple, objective and convenient way of supporting the Mosaic origin of the Sinaitic covenant and the Decalogue, and of refuting the separation of the Exodus and Sinai traditions[64] (all of which effect the evaluation of Eichrodt's *Theology*) has now become a point of critical contention.

The Hittite vassal treaties were considered unique with respect to their 'historical prologues' – reviews of the gracious acts of the suzerains which prepared the way for the treaty-relation. However, it has been denied that these prologues are unique to these treaties. Hittite parity treaties may include them, whilst an eighteenth-century treaty from Alalakh (although it has been questioned whether this is a proper treaty) and a seventh-century Assyrian treaty contain them.[65] In spite of these, it is still true that the use of historical prologues is characteristic of Hittite vassal treaties of the thirteenth and twelfth centuries, and in foundation treaties they may well be unique to them. Even so, closer examination of the accounts of the Sinaitic covenant has made it questionable whether 'historical prologues' occur there. But if they are not distinct is it because of the separation of the material from the cultic sphere in which the credos (historical prologues) would have been followed by laws? McCarthy, whose care and precision in analysing the treaties is to be commended, does less than justice to the position of people like Beyerlin when he criticizes them for seeing the whole of the treaty form where only a single element is present in the biblical material. Beyerlin argues that the biblical material developed from a cultic celebration which was similar to the treaties, so the fragmentation of the elements of the treaty form in the biblical material results from writing down the content of these celebrations as a narrative.[66]

The Hittite treaties also seemed to account for the second person singular negative apodictic commands found in the Decalogue and elsewhere.[67] Yet Gerstenberger and others have maintained that such commands are not to be related to any treaty concepts but to the clan ethos.[68] The biblical wisdom material is used to support this. However, as the commands include ritual matters and crimes of violence which are not dealt with in the wisdom material, and as the commands are con-

structed with *lō'* + imperfect and not as the wisdom maxims with
'al + jussive, which gives the commands a more emphatic form,
they may well be ultimately dependent on the Hittite treaty
forms.[69]

The use of the Hittite treaties to defend the historical connections between the Exodus and Sinai seems more dubious. Even if
Huffmon is right and the treaties themselves were not regarded as
gracious acts of the suzerain which ought to be included in the
historical prologues, there are references to previous treaties in
some prologues and therefore references to Sinai would be
expected in Josh. 24 and II Kings 22–23.[70]

International treaties have played an important part in the
evaluations of this early material in recent years. It is easy,
therefore, to think that Eichrodt's position stands or falls with this
issue. But such is not the case: Eichrodt developed his *Theology*
independently of it; even when the parallel with the Hittite
treaties is denied it is still possible to hold that the Sinaitic
narratives reflect a covenant relationship between Yahweh and
Israel. McCarthy, for instance, believes it was a covenant based on
rite and not treaty.

The evidence is overwhelming that there is a very strong cultic
element in the most antique presentations of Israel's special relationship,
its covenant relationship with Yahweh.[71]

Further, Zimmerli, whilst he is obviously aware of the Hittite
parallels, has proceeded independently of them, to argue that a
proper analysis of Ex. 19–34 shows that both the J and E Sinaitic
narratives presupposed that obligations were accepted by the
people as part of the covenant.[72] He argues against Begrich that
the covenant was not a matter of pure gift but neither was it a
matter of human obligations alone because the covenant presupposes God's gracious acts. In fact his analysis suggests a
similar situation to that envisaged by Eichrodt.

This article indicates the possibility that the earliest traditions
which we have of the Sinaitic covenant might differ fundamentally
in their conception of it. Eichrodt was not troubled by this
possibility because his theologizing was the result of reflecting
on the event which he thought lay behind the traditions.[73] But
others, especially M. Newman and J. R. Porter, have indicated that
there was a considerable divergence of understanding of the

Sinaitic covenant as the traditions developed and even in the earliest narratives.[74] Newman summarizes these as follows:

E is more congregational, democratic, prophetic and ethical. It reflects a kind of 'Kingdom of Priests' covenant theology. J is more priestly, cultic, authoritarian and dynastic in tendency. It reflects a 'dynastic' covenant theology.[75]

This introduces a new dimension to the problem as Eichrodt had seen it. This awareness of variety in the covenant concepts will be considered more fully in the next section.

In many ways, in spite of new material and new perspectives, the date of the Sinaitic covenant, as well as its nature and importance for Israel's faith, are as unsettled as when Eichrodt penned his *Theology*. The introduction of the idea of cultic festivals, held originally at Shechem and later transferred to Jerusalem, made it more conceivable that the covenant traditions could be so influential. The Hittite parallels made a Mosaic dating feasible and strikingly confirmed Eichrodt's theological deductions. The prophets appeared as defenders of a covenant relationship with Yahweh, which presupposed human obedience as detailed in the covenant laws, against an unfaithful and complacent Israel. Yet none of these issues has been finalized.

Eichrodt's *Theology*, then, has the advantage that its central subject is an important issue for both the OT itself and for modern investigations of the OT. Inevitably this means that the basis of his *Theology* is always in jeopardy because it is such a controversial subject. Yet, even those who do not accept Eichrodt's belief in a Mosaic covenant-making at Sinai, may still be able to value his *Theology*.[76]

For instance, those who regard Deuteronomy as the initiator of the covenant idea may consider that this involves not so much a change in theology (they may accept that for a long while Israel had regarded herself as Yahweh's people and Yahweh as her God) but rather a new and useful means of making the implications of her beliefs clear and, to some extent, consistent. Hence, Eichrodt's *Theology* might still serve to *illuminate* Israel's thinking for us (cf. I.13).[77] Or if they recognize, as this position surely must, the vast range of influence which the Deuteronomic school has had both on the Pentateuch and on the Former and the Later Prophets, then Eichrodt's *Theology* may be a useful guide to the OT text as understood within this tradition.[78] For those who value the OT as a record of revelation, this Deuteronomic view-point would be of great importance.

The position of those who believe that the covenant was important after the settlement for the life of the amphictyony is less difficult to reconcile with Eichrodt's *Theology*. Certainly they might question his claims about 'the factual nature of the divine revelation' and that 'faith in the covenant God assumes a remarkably interior attitude to history' (I. 37, 41), for these are deductions made on the assumption that the covenant is grounded on the Exodus events. But, as von Rad's *Theology* indicates, at least the second of these might be accepted on other grounds. Eichrodt allows for a broadening, deepening and even correcting of the Mosaic revelation, so there need be no great difference between his position and the one indicated above. This is especially the case where the joining of the supposedly distinct traditions of Sinai and Exodus is itself valued as part of the process of revelation.

On the other hand, those who accept the plausibility of a Mosaic covenant at Sinai, based on the Exodus events, need not follow Eichrodt's exposition. Closer attention to the text, in the light of both political and personal treaties, has emphasized the variety in the biblical traditions of the covenant of God with Israel; can it be accepted that the Mosaic understanding was as near the truth as Eichrodt thinks? Were those for whom the Sinaitic covenant was less important, and who may therefore have introduced other insights into God's nature which were contained in their traditions, of such insignificance, or did their insights play a valuable part in the development of the covenant traditions? We shall now consider one aspect of these issues which is particularly important for an evaluation of Eichrodt's *Theology*.

4. *How Many Covenants?*

Eichrodt regards the covenant between God and Israel, established at Sinai under Moses, as the fundamental basis of Israel's relationship with God. However, the OT knows of other divine-human covenants, the most important being the Abrahamic (Gen. 15; 17) which precedes the Sinaitic covenant, and the Davidic (II Sam. 7) which follows it. Eichrodt is aware of this (I. 53, 56f., 64) but he seems to denigrate these covenants in an unacceptable way. The whole patriarchal history, including the covenant with Abraham, is 'a remarkable retrojection of the covenant concept into the earliest period of the nation's life' (I. 49) and the Davidic covenant is regarded as a postscript to Sinai to which too much importance was given in the post-exilic period (I. 64). Even in his section on 'The Monarchy as a Religious Office in the History of the Covenant People', all he says of this covenant is:

The prophets . . . bestow the divine approval on his efforts to stabilize the kingdom, and promise that his dynasty shall endure for ever (I. 447).

When we examine the OT, it is quite clear that these two covenants were of great importance for the development of Israel's theology over a long period. Whilst there are few references to the Abrahamic covenant in pre-exilic prophets or psalms,[79] we know that this covenant was highly regarded by the Yahwist source of the Pentateuch. It also occurs frequently in Deuteronomy, the Deuteronomic History and P. Ezekiel 33 shows that it was an important element in the thought of ordinary Israelites around the time of the Exile. The Davidic covenant is mentioned in II Sam. 7 and Pss. 89 and 132, and dominates the work of the Chronicler. In neither case can the importance of these covenants be estimated merely by the *number* of references to them. Such references as we have indicate that these covenants were vital elements in the development, preservation and reapplication of Israel's faith at critical points in the nation's life, such as the transference to a monarchical government, the exile and the restoration. This importance is reflected in the structural and thematic positions which these covenants occupy in their sources. In the case of the Davidic covenant it was important for preserving the stability of the southern dynasty and fostering messianic hopes.[80]

The importance of these covenants cannot be restricted to the level of conceptions. Their importance and functions within the biblical traditions reflects the importance of the groups whose life and worship were influenced by these beliefs. It is possible that originally the Abrahamic covenant was the entitlement to part of Israel's territory, and that the Davidic covenant, even if it is not of Davidic origin, established the propriety of monarchic rule in Israel. So in both cases, but especially with the Davidic, these covenants were originally connected with important developments in Israel's life.[81]

It cannot be denied that these covenants were influential in a variety of OT 'schools' over long periods and at critical points in the development of Israel's theology. The question then arises, as to why Eichrodt allowed such a small part to them. To answer that it was because the concept of covenant which he had was univocal, i.e. the Sinaitic covenant, is only restating the problem. There are several factors which probably contributed to his position. When he wrote his *Theology* the importance of these covenants within their literary sources, within the traditions in which they developed and their contribution to Israel's life, worship and thought, was not as fully appreciated as it is to-day. Secondly, these covenants are with individuals and not with *Israel*. Eichrodt believes that Sinai is responsible for Israel's existence, thus the Abrahamic covenant is only anticipatory and the Davidic takes place within the framework of the Sinaitic covenant and should therefore be subordinate to it. Perhaps also, Eichrodt doubted whether he could establish the uniqueness of the concept of covenants between deities and individuals. Then, he does not appear to regard these covenants as historical, nor does he see in them the interpretation of history which is so crucial for his concept of revelation. But the most important reason is that Eichrodt saw in these covenants a type of relationship with God to which he was fundamentally opposed because it was unconditional and claimed eternal validity. If these reasons, to some extent, account for Eichrodt's treatment of the Abrahamic and Davidic covenants, none of them, least of all the last, justifies it. To see this we shall now examine the nature of these covenants.

In some respects we can consider the Abrahamic and Davidic covenants together. The earliest account of the Abrahamic covenant is in the Yahwist source, where it appears as an essential element. There is much evidence to suggest that it was written to account for Israel's position reached through David's reign, therefore it has a similar purpose to the Davidic covenant. There are also reasons for thinking that these two covenants may have had a mutual influence.[82] Indeed, David's rise to power and his conquest of Jerusalem was probably responsible for bringing the Abrahamic covenant to its position of importance within *Israel*.

David could have come into contact with it during his rule at Hebron; then, when he became king of all Israel, these local traditions became Israel's heirloom.[83] However, the most important reason for linking them is that the covenants appear to be of a similar type, in comparison with the Sinaitic one. The latter is a vassal type treaty, conditioned by law, made with the nation, and because of its conditional nature, of uncertain duration. The former are promissory covenants, made with individuals, without conditions and therefore of eternal validity.[84] Thus Eichrodt could see in them a threat to the 'real' covenant relationship, because the eternal validity and unconditional nature of the promises appeared to bind God to Israel, fostering self-satisfaction and complacency and neglecting the essential element of Israel's religious and moral response of obedience and depriving her beliefs of any eschatological thrust. If we can no longer belittle the importance of the Abrahamic and Davidic covenants as Eichrodt did, does his *Theology* become an anachronism? It would seem to be difficult to integrate a second, distinct type of covenant into his *Theology*. But, are these two covenant types as distinct as most accounts suggest?[85]

Let us consider some minor points first. The Sinaitic covenant can also be presented in the form of a promise,[86] whilst the historical prologue finds a place in the Abrahamic and Davidic covenants.[87] True, the Abrahamic and Davidic covenants are with individuals, but there is evidence that they were 'democratized'.[88] Further, both these covenants involve the whole nation: Abraham's seed is to become a 'great nation', and from the extent of the land (J) and the rite of circumcision (P) it is clear that this nation is Israel; the 'Promise to David' includes 'a place for my people Israel'; conversely, Ex. 24.1–2, 9–11 considers that the human partner of the Sinaitic covenant is Moses (possibly Aaron, Nadab and Abihu as well) although Israel is implicated by the individual.[89]

From Eichrodt's position, it would seem that it is the lack of conditions and the eternal validity of the covenant which is the main problem. The first point to realize is that these do not necessarily entail one another. Both II Sam. 7.16 and Ps. 89.28f. clearly state that the Davidic covenant is 'for ever'. Equally, these passages imply that the relationship involved the obedience of the covenant members to Yahweh (II Sam. 7.16; Ps. 89.30f.).

These covenants are eternal not because there are no conditions but because God is going to ensure that the conditions are kept. The difference between this conception and that of Ps. 132 is that in the former cases God is going to correct disobedience and in the latter he is going to reject the disobedient people (cf. Ps. 132.12), thus ending the covenant relationship.[90]

That conditions and eternal validity are not antithetical is indicated by Ex. 32.10. This passage occurs in the Golden Calf episode, which suggests that the Sinaitic covenant was certainly regarded as conditional. This verse, however, implies that God will keep his covenant even though his conditions have been broken, but he will do this by using a different group to achieve his purpose: 'Let me alone, that my wrath may burn hot against them and I may consume them; but of you I will make a great nation.' Appeal is often made to Ex. 32.13f. to show that P, in the face of the tragedy of the exile, wanted to ground the covenant in the unconditional promise to the patriarchs,[91] but Ex. 32.10 shows that even a conditional covenant could be eternal.

Once it is realized that belief in the eternal nature of the covenant did not necessarily imply that the relationship was unconditional, it is possible to re-examine the Abrahamic and Davidic covenants for evidence of their conditional nature. To start with, it is extremely probable that the original form of the Abrahamic covenant involved some conditions even if these were not stated.[92] Certainly, the Yahwist mentions no obligations (Gen. 15.7–21), but within the Yahwist's presentation Abraham has already responded with obedience to Yahweh's command to leave his own country (Gen. 12.1–3) and even here he obeys Yahweh's commands (Gen. 15.9ff.). Thus, it is by no means clear that the Yahwist thought of the covenant as unconditional, in the sense that God would have made the promise and would keep it whatever Abraham did, or decided to do.[93] Furthermore, it is quite illegitimate to neglect the conditional nature of the Abrahamic covenant in P (Gen. 17). The giving of the covenant is preceded by a far-reaching command, 'Walk before me and be blameless' (Gen. 17.1), which appears to be the condition for the giving of the covenant. Abraham accepts this condition when he bows before God. Again, the validity of this covenant is specifically stated to depend on circumcision: 'Every male among you shall be circumcised', and this covenant must be 'kept' (Gen.

17.10). Failure to obey involves rejection by God and exclusion from the promise. Clements says that circumcision is 'interpreted as the *sign* of its institution and validity',[94] but care must be taken to distinguish this from the rainbow, the *sign* of the Noachic covenant (Gen.9.12). The rainbow is from start to finish God's act (Gen.9.13, 15), circumcision is from start to finish man's responsibility (Gen.17.11). There is no indication whatsoever that anyone can be rejected from the Noachic covenant. It is truly unconditional in a way that the Abrahamic covenant is not. In the exilic period, circumcision indicated membership of the people of God, which implied a certain pattern of behaviour and distinctiveness within a foreign culture. Circumcision implied 'restrictive conditions' which should not be contrasted with the Sinai law covenant.[95]

Equally, considerations of the Davidic covenant show that it is not easy to accept that it was unconditional. II Sam.7 mentions no obligations, but it does assume the obedience of David to Yahweh's demand that he desist from building the temple.[96] Further, if, as is probable, this passage developed with the 'royal ritual', then the king had to accept the obligations laid on him by Yahweh within that ceremony before he received the covenant promise.[97] So although the covenants are of formally distinct types, this does not mean that the theological understandings expressed by the Sinaitic covenant could not be expressed by the Davidic and Abrahamic.

We should also remember that these covenants are not only conceptually similar but are also linked within the biblical traditions. This suggests that they can be understood in relationship to one another rather than in isolation or even opposition. In J and P the Abrahamic covenant is integrated with the Sinaitic and II Sam.7 is closely related to the bringing of the ark to Jerusalem, with which the Sinaitic traditions were linked. Of course, there are varying estimates of the way these covenants were understood within the different traditions. With J, some think that the Abrahamic covenant is a 'preparatory' stage and Sinai the fulfilment, whilst others claim Sinai had only minor significance.[98] With P, there is the problem of whether it was intended to dominate the other traditions or to supplement them. It has been argued that P does not consider Sinai to be a covenant at all but rather the means by which the promises given to Abraham are fulfilled; by treating it in this way it was possible to emphasize the grace element in Israel's relationship to God in the exilic period, at a time when some believed that the exile meant that Israel's covenant was annulled through her disobedience.[99] Yet, with P, the Abrahamic covenant is not unconditional, and the P account of Sinai is best understood as the exposition of what it meant to 'walk blamelessly' before God.

De Vaux has argued that there are many indications that the king was considered a vassal of Yahweh, just as the kings of the subject nations in a vassal treaty.[100] This claim has been contested by McCarthy, who argues that all the elements cited as evidence by de Vaux can be accounted for without recourse to the vassal treaties.[101] Nevertheless, as McCarthy acknowledges that the king was considered Yahweh's vassal, de Vaux has provided us with a way of seeing how the Davidic covenant could have been, and probably was, integrated with the Sinaitic treaty.

Chronicles is often thought to be the final development of the Davidic covenant at the expense of the Sinaitic. But this is a dubious estimate. To start with, there is the problem of whether Chronicles says little about Moses and the Exodus because it accepts the Pentateuch as canonical or because it wishes to correct it.[102] Certainly, Chronicles does concentrate on David rather than Moses, but this was appropriate because the Davidic dynasty had greatly affected Israel's political, social and religious life. However, Chronicles certainly knows of the Sinaitic covenant.[103] The ark contains 'the covenant of the Lord which he made with the children of Israel' (II Chron. 6.11) and 'There was nothing in the ark save two tables that Moses put there at Horeb, when the Lord made a covenant with the children of Israel when they came out of Egypt' (II Chron. 5.10).

Perhaps the most serious problem which Chronicles presents is the claim that it omits any conditions to the Davidic covenant and so heightens its promissory nature. North says, 'II Chron. 6.10 omits the conditions and threats added in II Sam. 7.14.'[104] To be precise, II Chron. 6.10 is parallel to I Kings 8.20 which also lacks these conditions. Anyway, II Chron. 6.14, 16 show that this covenant was understood to be conditional. The real parallel to II Sam. 7.14 is I Chron. 17.13 where, it is true, the conditions are missing. But in the light of I Chron. 28.9, 10, which states clearly that Solomon's position was conditional on his obedience, not too much should be made of the lacuna in I Chron. 17.13 – all the more so, because there is no parallel to I Chron. 28.9, 10 in Kings, so presumably it is the creation of the Chronicler. Finally, the theory of retribution, for which Chronicles is so often criticized, assumes that the promises of God are conditioned by human obedience. Thus, in spite of II Chron. 6.10, Chronicles knows of the Sinaitic covenant and understands the Davidic covenant to be conditional.

It is possible to account for the mutual influence of the Abrahamic and Davidic covenants through an initial contact brought about by David's stay at Hebron prior to his rise to power in Israel. In a similar way, the Sinaitic and Abrahamic/Davidic covenants came together when David brought the ark to Jerusalem and gave it a position of authority, for the ark is connected with the Sinaitic traditions.[105] This does not mean that the Abrahamic/Davidic covenants have not modified the OT picture of God's relationship with Israel, but rather that some of these modifications have been registered within the development of the Sinaitic covenant traditions. So, even if the two were originally of distinct formal types they should not be placed in antithesis, all the more because the OT itself is concerned to integrate them.[106] This means that the recognition of the importance of the Abrahamic and Davidic covenants for Israel's religion, theology and history does not invalidate Eichrodt's approach, even though this is based on the Sinaitic covenant. The dangers which Eichrodt would see in the apparently unconditional and eternal nature of the Abrahamic and Davidic covenants is minimized when the historical situations, which necessitated the integration of these covenants with the Sinaitic, are recalled. These covenants represent an enrichment of Israel's covenant theology which ought to modify Eichrodt's *Theology* in the ways indicated below.

It must be emphasized that in spite of recognizing the importance of the Abrahamic/Davidic covenants, the Sinaitic covenant should be given pride of place. There is both historical and theological justification for this. Secondly, we should remember that it is only the Yahwist who narrates an unconditional Abrahamic covenant. But, both from the context and from the way this covenant is integrated with the Sinaitic, it must be doubted whether he regarded Abraham's (or Israel's) relation to God as unconditional. Thirdly, as David himself may have been responsible for linking the Sinaitic covenant with his kingship, these two covenants should be considered in tandem rather than opposition. Although the monarchy may have been the supreme reality for some in Israel, it was never independent of its pre-monarchic foundations. Thus both covenant types correspond to a real 'life-force' in Israel and these were probably expressed in and fostered by the cultic celebrations which celebrated these covenants. Fourthly, it is important to note that when Israel's theologians wished to express the significance of the monarchy and its place in the total life of Israel, they did this by means of a covenant between God and king, and through the king with the people. This confirms Eichrodt's belief in the importance of covenant for Israel's thinking.

In view of the above considerations, Eichrodt needs a more favourable estimate of the monarchy at the historical level. Theologically, it is necessary to compare the differences in the Abrahamic, Sinaitic and Davidic covenant conceptions and to estimate the importance of these for different groups within Israel. It would also be necessary to show how the Abrahamic and Davidic covenants enabled Israel to re-express her covenant theology in the changed politico-religious situations brought about by the monarchy, as well as considering their value in the periods of the exile and restoration. Whilst this would make deep inroads into the exalted position given to the Sinaitic covenant it would enable him to show more clearly that 'living process' for which covenant is the code-word.

Conclusions
In this chapter we have shown how important the covenant concept is for Eichrodt's *Theology*, for the OT and for modern OT scholarship. We have indicated that its real meaning for Eichrodt is the divine–human relationship embodied in the OT accounts of the covenant at Sinai. Thus, the centre of his *Theology* is an issue which is as much in debate to-day as when he published his *Theology*. We have argued that he has not given sufficient attention to the Abrahamic and Davidic covenants. However, although this means that his *Theology* needs to be modified, these other covenants should enrich rather than destroy his position.

III

VON RAD'S THEOLOGY: HEILSGESCHICHTE

We have already indicated that *Heilsgeschichte* (saving or salvation history)[1] is the central and critical issue of von Rad's *Theology*.[2] Because he makes this the subject of his *Theology* he uses it to distinguish his *Theology* from other types. It also serves in the justification of its organization, the characterization of the main unique feature of Israel's faith, the connection between the historical and prophetic traditions and the linking of the OT to the NT. Later, we shall investigate his *Theology* by considering the claims which he makes for *Heilsgeschichte*, but first, we must try and clarify the meaning of *Heilsgeschichte* in his *Theology*.

1. *The Meaning of* Heilsgeschichte *for von Rad*

Von Rad acknowledges that the term is not his own creation (II. vi, 362). It goes back to J. C. K. von Hofmann who, in giving priority to the biblical history as a theological form, was influenced by Coccejus and Bengel.[3] Von Rad distinguished his understanding from Hofmann's and others with a similar use like Beck and Delitzsch because they were interested in an 'objective saving history' which von Rad claimed, 'does not derive from the OT'[4] (II. vi). This separation of the 'objective history' of scientific research and salvation history is fundamental to von Rad's Theology and it has far reaching repercussions. In taking over a term which had a fairly specific meaning and reminting it for his own purpose, von Rad increases the difficulty of arriving at a clear understanding of what he means by *Heilsgeschichte*. So far as I am aware he has never defined exactly what he meant by it.[5] He admits that he is unhappy with the term, it is 'a dangerous cipher' and he has considered trying to find 'a new word for our concern'.[6]

That its meaning is not clear is indicated by a number who have written about *Heilsgeschichte* and have connections with von Rad's *Theology*. Keller concludes that von Rad means by it, 'the *method of research* which investigates the history of traditions', whereas Koch defines it as 'a complex *literary type*'. C. Barth believes that for von Rad it is 'a successively *developing sequence of events* in the history of Israel and the nations'. J. A. Soggin uses it to summarize 'what the great works of history in the OT and the whole of the NT had already *asserted about the past* which was *formed* fundamentally *by God's operation*'. Baumgärtel, who senses von Rad's lack of precision, considers that it is 'where the past facts are experienced as powerful for salvation' that we have *Heilsgeschichte*.[7] This lack of consistency in secondary opinion suggests we should consult von Rad.

In his *Theology* there are some explicit indications as to what he means by *Heilsgeschichte*. It can refer to the series of events which Israel used to explain her arrival in Canaan, 'the "canonical" saving history, from the patriarchs down to the entry into Canaan' (I. 126). In close connection with this it is 'definite election traditions' (I. 69, cf. II. 303). Then, there are a number of similar theological explanations. It is 'a history created by Yahweh' (I. 70), 'a history with Yahweh' (I. 91), 'the divine history with Israel' (I. 126), 'what takes place between Israel and Yahweh' (I. 328), or, 'the history of Israel's dealings with Yahweh' (II. 226). Von Rad recognizes that within the OT there are different understandings of *Heilsgeschichte* of which the most important seems to be that of the Deuteronomic historian. Other views are provided by Josh. 2–10 or David's rise to power. Sometimes it is understood as a meta-historical view-point, an understanding of the dimension of history (cf. II. 110f.), elsewhere it is linked with revelation, 'that revelation of Yahweh's will which was pre-eminently turned towards Israel' (I. 450), or 'that . . . interconnexion between divine word and historical acts' (II. 382). These descriptions of *Heilsgeschichte* confirm that, as von Rad uses it, it has a wide scope and rather imprecise meaning, for they are not all on the same logical or conceptual level. Of course, words do tend to spread their meaning ('meaning' and 'history' are prime examples), but with *Heilsgeschichte* this causes problems in von Rad's *Theology*.

For instance, when von Rad writes, 'The exile was a period devoid of saving history' (I.126), does he mean that from it no election traditions developed, or that God was not creating Israel's history, or that God had nothing to do with Israel, or that Israel believed God had nothing to do with her? A number of contradictory statements suggest that even von Rad himself does not know what he means. He claims that Ecclesiasticus 44–50 is 'the first example of the history of Israel presented without reference to the saving history' (II.306), but also that the concept of wisdom here has enabled 'the wisdom teaching to draft a tremendous scheme of world and saving history' (I.445, cf. I.327). Again, 'the prophetic message is specifically rooted in the saving history' (II.303), yet, the prophets' conviction 'places them basically outside the saving history . . .' (I.128). Further, at II.110, saving history is an understanding of the dimension of history, whereas at II.412 this understanding seems to be something additional to the saving history. Finally, the salvation history is 'the bed-rock fact in Israel's way of looking at history . . . she held on to this right to the end' (II.426). But the literature of the later period such as post-exilic legalism, wisdom, scepticism, and apocalyptic are all criticized because they had given up this salvation history understanding (I.91, 349, 354, 433, 455, II.303, 308) which suggests that Israel did not hold on to it 'right to the end'. If von Rad is confused by his own term then the reader must expect difficulties too.

There are two passages which appear to offer hopes of clarification: one positively, telling us what a 'clear formulation' of *Heilsgeschichte* is; the other negatively, telling us of material which lacks it completely and from which we should therefore be able to deduce what is not. Von Rad maintains:

This Deuteronomic theology of history was the first which clearly formulated the phenomenon of saving history,[8] that is of a course of history which was shaped and led to a fulfilment by a word of judgment and salvation continually injected into it (I.344).[9]

By 'clear formulation' perhaps no more is implied than that this is a 'consistent account' or a 'clear account', but M. Honecker has argued that

So far as von Rad's own understanding of history is systematically and theologically articulated it aligns itself most plainly and clearly with the

Deuteronomic view of history.[10]

There is an element of truth in this claim even though von Rad does acknowledge that other events were included in the *Heilsgeschichte*, different significance was seen in the same events and different groups could view the same period differently.[11] However, even if the Deuteronomic view corresponded exactly to von Rad's position this would not take us very far, because the Deuteronomic view is not all that clear. Such clarity as it has relates more to the means by which this history was brought about than any understanding of the history itself. Further, it is extremely difficult to know what the 'later formulations' might be since nearly all the later material lacks this *Heilsgeschichte*, according to von Rad.[12] Indeed, if he were right it would seem that once clarity had been achieved the idea was rejected! So, for a variety of reasons, this passage is not as helpful as we might hope.

The second, negative clarification, relates to Ecclus. 44–50:

Here . . . is to be found the first example of the history of Israel presented without reference to the saving history and merely as a catalogue of the events concerned (II. 306).[13]

Elsewhere, von Rad claimed that it was characteristic of the saving history to recapitulate the main events, 'with close concentration on the objective historical facts' (I. 122) which seems similar to a 'catalogue of the events'.[14] However, this passage implies that nothing in Ecclus. 44–50 can count as saving history. This claim merely adds to our confusion, in view of the many references to God's activity in history, for instance in the story of Joshua:

For the Lord himself brought his enemies unto him . . . He called upon the Most High . . . and the great Lord heard him. With hailstones of mighty power he caused war to break violently upon the nations (Ecclus. 46.3–6; cf. 44.1f., 21, 25; 45.3,6; 46.9,10,18; 47.13,25).

Certainly, God's activity appears more indirect here than in some parts of the OT, partly because it is closely linked with important individuals and partly because God acts in response to the appeal of men. In both respects Ecclesiasticus is nearer to Chronicles than to the Deuteronomic history which von Rad so admires.

But, rather than any denial of God's activity or rejection of salvation history, Ecclesiasticus is surely an alternative understanding of it.

Many of the constituent events of the saving history are also mentioned here, such as the promise to the patriarchs, the entry into Canaan, Sinai and the covenant with David. Other events not in the 'canonical' saving history are also included, such as the division of the kingdom (47.24–31), the exile of the northern tribes (45.15ff.) etc. True, little is made of the Exodus event (cf.45.2), but references to many of the events of the saving history make it difficult to understand von Rad's position. Later, von Rad claimed:

The concern here is not concern with the obvious or the hidden examples of God's guidance . . . nor with the relationship of tension between promise and fulfilment. . . .[15]

But the oath to Abraham (44.21–23) and the covenant with David are important. Further, God is intent on fulfilling his promises such as those made to Joshua and Caleb (note the purposive infinitive). In spite of the people's sin, 'The Lord would not go back on his mercy or undo any of his words' (47.22, Jerusalem Bible). Thus, rather than showing what *Heilsgeschichte* is not, we feel that Ecclus.44–50 shows that von Rad's opinion of this passage is incorrect and his concept of *Heilsgeschichte* confused. If these chapters do lack all reference to the *Heilsgeschichte* it is extremely difficult to know what the word can mean.[16]

However we try and clarify the meaning of *Heilsgeschichte* in von Rad's *Theology*, we are left with the uncomfortable feeling that it does not have any clear or uniform meaning. General divisions of meaning and guesses as to its connotations in specific contexts can be made, but this does not seem adequate when we recall the important functions it has and the strong claims which are made for it in this *Theology*. As we now proceed to examine these points its imprecision must be borne in mind.

2. The Functions of Heilsgeschichte in von Rad's Theology

Von Rad wishes to make a complete distinction between his type of Theology, based on the *Heilsgeschichte*, and the normal type which aims to construct Israel's 'world of faith'. Although some of his statements about this are ambivalent (cf. I.vi, 105, 111, 114, 120, II.vif.)[17] he really makes an exclusive claim for his own approach.[18] His justification for this is that his procedure corresponds to the nature of the OT, therefore his claims for *Heilsgeschichte* are not only about his *Theology* but also the OT itself. There seem to be five main reasons for his position, although these are so interrelated that it is not possible to present them as a logical progression. They are:

(*a*) OT Theology should restrict itself to Israel's 'explicit assertions' about Yahweh, that is to say to the kerygma, which is the *Heilsgeschichte*.

(*b*) This subject, in contrast to the 'world of faith', provides the theologian with a 'unique' subject.

(*c*) Israel's *Heilsgeschichte* has something valid to say about the reality of history, it is not merely a matter of abstract ideas. The normal type of Theology cannot do justice to this fact.

(*d*) Only a saving history Theology enables the prophetic and historical traditions to be integrated in an appropriate way.

(*e*) Only a saving history Theology provides us with a proper understanding of the relationship between the Testaments, as the real connection is in fact a saving history one.

We shall now examine the implications and validity of these points.

(*a*) *Old Testament Theology should be restricted to the* Heilsgeschichte. Von Rad's desire to restrict OT Theology to the kerygma was conditioned by the general theological climate in which his *Theology* was formed and by his analysis of the Hexateuch. He believed that this was built up around a few basic historical events, as indicated by the 'small credo' of Deut. 26.5ff. However, it is difficult to see how any legitimate NT Theology could restrict itself to the 'kerygma' and ignore the 'didache', and it is equally difficult for the OT. Indeed, von Rad was forced to admit that the OT material was not as restricted as he first claimed. In the first edition he stated:

The OT writings confine themselves to representing Yahweh's relationship to Israel and the world in one aspect only, namely as a continuing divine activity in history (I. 106).

But later he acknowledge that the OT mentions much more, including men, offices and cultic usages (I. 114f. is an addition to the first German edition). Further, it proved impossible to restrict his task to 're-telling', 'without becoming obscure' (I. 121). Thus, von Rad cannot do justice either to the OT or to his readers if he restricts himself as he would like to do. There are even occasions when he rejects the *Heilsgeschichte* whilst holding on to the theology (I. 349).

The apparent advantage of dealing only with 'explicit assertions' is that these would enable him to avoid the inferences without which the 'world of faith' could not be constructed and thereby also avoid the 'problematic nature' of what claims to be theology. In fact, von Rad can do no such thing. The 'explicit assertions' also involve inferences at a number of levels: not only that of written word to meaning, but also of what is important (e.g. 'the most important aspect theologically' I. 335) and the traditions on which any passage depends and without which it cannot be understood (cf. II. 225). Such background 'lies concealed' as much as Israel's faith (cf. I. 111).

Perhaps the most serious issue is that von Rad's claims are just not valid for the whole of the OT. This point has been forcibly made by J. Barr,[19] who insists rightly that a substantial portion of the OT does not suggest that revelation is through history, or that *Heilsgeschichte* alone is of value. He mentions the wisdom material, many psalms and Israel's understanding of creation.[20] Von Rad himself admits this for post-exilic legal piety (I. 91) and apocalyptic (II. 303f.). Barr says that Job and Ecclesiastes show that 'there is a valid talking about God which does not work by a constant reference to a historical datum'.[21] Von Rad does not omit reference to this material, but he uses its independence from saving history to explain why such material fails to deal with the problems of faith which concerned it. 'This very lack is closely connected with the grave affliction which is the theme of both these works' (I. 106). Barr does not really explain von Rad's procedure. From II. 417 it seems that von Rad believed that in re-telling the *Heilsgeschichte* the OT shows how 'more precise positive and negative evaluations (are) to be made'; thus, theological evaluations can be made from within the OT by accepting the *Heilsgeschichte* as the norm. Not only is this a circular argument (i.e. the OT is really about *Heilsgeschichte*, therefore anything in it which is not must be interpreted negatively),[22] but it is also inadequate from within the OT. The prophets show that even

when there was a strong emphasis on the saving history understood as election guaranteeing Israel's well being, there could still
be problems for those who held such a faith as well as in that
faith itself. The prophets insisted that the *Heilsgeschichte* must be
properly understood if sense were to be made of contemporary
political events which threatened Israel's faith. So *Heilsgeschichte*
did not guarantee correct theology, nor did belief in it guarantee
there would be no problems for the faith of the believer.

This concentration on the *Heilsgeschichte* as the standard by
which everything is to be measured also leads to false presentation
of the OT material.[23] Barr has argued that this is the case for
'creation'.[24] C. Barth has queried the legitimacy of treating the
psalms as Israel's response, because the Hexateuch is equally an
expression of Israel's response, especially when, as with von Rad
himself, its cultic origins are emphasized.[25] Again, von Rad had
to admit that some of the psalms are not even the response to the
Heilsgeschichte, for their theme is 'the action of Yahweh in nature'
(I. 360).[26] It seems to me that von Rad's views about apocalyptic
literature are equally unacceptable. He emphasizes the connection
between wisdom and apocalyptic traditions and denies the
connection with prophecy. He does this by maintaining that the
crucial issue is that apocalyptic lacks any connection with
Heilsgeschichte:

The prophetic message is specifically rooted in the saving history. . . .
But there is no way which leads from this to the apocalyptic view of
history . . . we may even ask whether apocalyptic literature had any
existential relationship with history at all, since it had abandoned the
approach by way of the saving history (II. 303f.).[27]

But if their views, even their vews of history, are evaluated other
than in terms of saving history, then important connections can
be seen.[28] Both believe in the final sovereignty of God.[29] The
determinism which von Rad stresses must be balanced by
apocalyptic's interest in 'the problem of human freedom'[30] and
can be properly considered an extension of the prophets' belief
'in the divine control of history and in the divine initiative in
history'.[31] Von Rad sees another distinction in the unitary view
of history found in apocalyptic. Elsewhere he admits that this
tendency appears in the prophets (II. 200, 242, 244, 343) and if
apocalyptic takes this a stage further does it not correspond to an

existential necessity as a result of the world horizons which were forced on it?[32] Von Rad implies that apocalyptic was more pessimistic than prophecy, seeing evil as an expression of the nature of man and not, as prophecy did, as 'the direct intervention of Yahweh in history' (II.305). Again, is this not also a consequence of the existential relationship with the history of its time? Prophecy too recognizes the human side of evil and at times blackens the past history to point more strongly to God's activity in the future, and in this it is not dissimilar to apocalyptic. Again, von Rad sees in apocalyptic's 'veiled standpoint' a divergence from prophecy. This was nothing new in Israel, we need only mention the Hexateuch and Deutero-Isaiah. Anyway, the standpoint of the apocalyptists may have been quite clear to their readers.[33] Thus, it is difficult to accept that von Rad has disproved the relationship between prophecy and apocalyptic.

Von Rad's own case depends largely on the supposedly 'encyclopaedic' nature of both apocalyptic and wisdom. But as Koch points out this is really true only for I Enoch in apocalyptic, and in this case, the apocalyptic origins of all the material are dubious.[34] Von Rad has also underestimated the dissimilarities of these traditions. In apocalyptic eschatology plays a central role, but it is absent from wisdom.[35] Wisdom is concerned with the individual of any nation whereas apocalyptic is more concerned with the nations and especially Israel. Again, the origins of apocalyptic material are found in the prophetic corpus (e.g. Isa. 25–27, Zechariah, and Joel).[36]

In fact, there seems little reason for following von Rad's claim that apocalyptic developed solely out of wisdom material and has no vital connections with prophecy. No one denies that apocalyptic differs from prophecy and one of the differences may be in the influence of some aspects of wisdom material, but this is no new idea.[37] Thus von Rad's estimate of apocalyptic is falsified by his evaluation of it in terms of its relation to *Heilsgeschichte*.

Von Rad's evaluation of everything by its relationship to the saving history is clearly dubious for several reasons. First, the whole argument is circular. Secondly, even if the *Heilsgeschichte* is unique to Israel there is no reason why other facets of her beliefs should be rejected just because they are not unique. Thirdly, it leads him to a negative theological judgment on material which he considers lacks this saving history connection and for this there is no real justification. Fourthly, on many occasions it results in dubious scholarship, as we have shown for apocalyptic.

Even when von Rad is dealing with parts of the OT which are connected with *Heilsgeschichte* his position is contestable. Barr points out that the paradigms for the 'history-centred picture of revelation' do not support the emphasis on God's acts, for in the OT 'these acts fall into a sequence with divine words and with human acts and human words'.[38] It is true that the verbal communication is given 'historical localization', but the importance of this is variable. G. E. Wright claims that Barr has oversimplified von Rad's position because his proper subject is 'the revelation in word and deed of Yahweh in history' (I. 114).[39] But, although von Rad has a section on 'The Prophets' Conception of the Word of God' (II. 8off.), indubitably his normal emphasis is on the divine acts (e.g. I. 113). It is acts which receive priority as the following passage shows:

Israel too, the object of this event [sc. the deliverance from Egypt], is silent. But when the tellers of the story come to describe it, they introduce a plethora of words, some allegedly spoken by Yahweh and some by Israel. Important as these are, the event which took place still remains the basic thing that happened. This datum ancient Israel never spiritualised (I. 176).

Now, why is 'allegedly' used of words but not divine acts? The events are 'allegedly' events not to mention their 'alleged' performance by Yahweh. Again, the Exodus 'event' included acts and words but von Rad contrasts these. Then, why does 'the event . . . remain the basic thing'? Possibly because all the material mentions it, but this is hardly surprising when the criterion for relevant material is just that.[40] Finally, it is extremely difficult to know what is meant by Israel 'never spiritualized' these events, since von Rad tells us how she interpreted them in various ways (cf. I. 177).

Further evidence for the priority of act over word is provided by the order in which von Rad expounds his material. The OT pattern is 'The Revelation of the Name of Yahweh' and then the Exodus, but von Rad reverses this, implying, unconsciously perhaps, that the revelation is through the event. Von Rad could defend his presentation if he were prepared to give up his claim to re-tell the biblical story.[41] Or he could argue that in the cult it was the recital of 'acts' which was primary, as Deut. 26.5ff. etc. shows. But Barr and others contest this form-critical position.[42] Even if it is accepted there is another problem. The original *Sitz im Leben* for such credos was the cult and the festivals. But this cultic environment included words of Yahweh through prophets and priests and words of human response in the hymns. Thus, these 'acts' may always have been in a verbal context. So, consideration of the pre-literary context of these credos might well involve a revision of von Rad's claims for the importance of 'acts'. Anyway, if the narrators introduce a 'plethora of words', presumably they thought they were important, so their importance should not be minimized by any re-teller! Thus, even when von Rad is dealing with the saving history material he over-estimates the importance of 'acts', or, if one prefers to put it so, he misrepresents the comprehensive nature of the 'divine events' for which words are as important as deeds.

We conclude that von Rad's setting of the *Heilsgeschichte* over against the 'world of faith' is illegitimate. Much of the OT is not as restricted to the acts of God as von Rad implies. His concentration on the *Heilsgeschichte* leads to a false evaluation of parts of the OT, if not all of it. The *Heilsgeschichte*, on any reasonable ground, belongs to 'the world of faith' and cannot be isolated from it. Anyway, an OT Theology which was really restricted to the *Heilsgeschichte* would have to ignore a great deal of the OT for which it is not central.

(b) The uniqueness of the Heilsgeschichte

One of von Rad's objections to OT Theologies which deal with Israel's 'world of faith' is that this has 'a thousand threads tying it closely to the world of the ancient Near East' (I. 113) so that it can be dealt with by 'orientalists, sociologists, ethnologists', etc. (I. 105). This implies that the theologian really needs a unique subject. It is not accidental, then, that the subject which von Rad considers to be the only legitimate subject for an OT Theology he also considers to be unique to Israel:

this idea of history made a radical division between Israel and her environment . . . with her idea of saving history she completely parted company with these religions (II. 110, cf. I. 116).

But, even if this *Heilsgeschichte* were unique, von Rad's position would still be unacceptable because orientalists, etc. are prepared to deal with distinctive view-points[43] and there is no reason why they should not do so. So again, the apparent distinction between 'world of faith' and 'saving history' breaks down.

However, the uniqueness of the *Heilsgeschichte* itself must be questioned. It is unique in the sense that many of the events are only referred to in the OT, but this is not unusual either for events or records of events. Secondly, in comparison with the ancient Near East the length of time eventually spanned in the *Heilsgeschichte* is unusual. Neither of these means that Israel had any special methodology or understanding of the nature of history, although it is in these ways that von Rad thinks the *Heilsgeschichte* is unique. These points have been carefully investigated by B. Albrektson, on whose research our criticism of von Rad's position largely depends.[44]

Von Rad claims that the sacral understanding of the world is non-historical and has no place for once-for-all events. The question then arises how Israel could unite the two in her cultic celebrations and also how in the 'cyclic' mythology of the religions of the ancient Near East it was possible to believe in the intervention of the gods in history.[45] Von Rad realized that the chronological concept of linear historical time must have clashed with the cultic view, but he does not see that the incorporation of the saving events in the cult meant that to some extent they lost their once-for-all nature.[46]

We may grant some validity to von Rad's generalization that it was the 'cyclical order of nature on which the ancient peoples of the east conferred the dignity of divinity' (II. 110), but the necessary qualifications are equally important. For this did not mean that with such deities the 'only sphere of activity is necessarily nature', nor were they limited to acting in or identified with that special aspect of nature with which they were customarily associated,[47] although von Rad implies these things. His presentation is misleading because for the ancient Near East he works with cultic material and brushes aside other views, whilst for the OT the cultic view is modified by the literature of the OT as well as pushed to one side by von Rad (cf. II. 320).

In fact, Albrektson found that it was impossible to distinguish Israel's view of history from that of the ancient Near East in any simple way. For both, history, including miraculous and ordinary events, was regarded as the sphere of divine activity.[48] In both historical events were regarded as a medium of revelation and the content of this revelation in history was similarly restricted to the power, mercy and wrath of the deities.[49] He also showed that it is incorrect to maintain that the ancient Near East's view of history was cyclic. Thus, the cyclic element of the cult did not, as von Rad assumed, come 'quite automatically to prominence' in such realms (cf. II. 111).[50]

The most that can be salvaged is that the *Heilsgeschichte* might be unique because history played a more important part in Israel's thinking about God and that it was God's acts in history rather than, though not to the exclusion of, nature which she believed guaranteed her well-being. As Albrektson says,

It would seem that the idea of historical events as divine manifestations has marked the Israelite cult in a way that lacks real parallels among Israel's neighbours. . . . The distinctiveness is not, however, found in the conception as such but in its relative importance, its capacity for influencing the cult.[51]

Although there are striking features such as its length and the effect on the cult, it is difficult to maintain that Israel's *Heilsgeschichte* is unique. A further difference might be that Israel's account kept nearer to actual happenings than was usual in the rest of the ancient Near East,[52] but von Rad cannot really consider this because of his methodological separation of the biblical from the critical pictures of her history.

Von Rad's views not only depend upon an unacceptable selection of material on which comparisons are made but also on an extremely confusing discussion of 'time', 'event' and 'history'. Rendtorff properly considers II Part 1 G to be 'the pivotal point of the whole work'[53] but it is also the most confusing. The concepts we have just mentioned are all 'slippery' and von Rad does not succeed in handling them. For instance, a cyclic view of time is not incompatible with a linear view of history, nor does the recognition that some events recur mean that history is cyclic, etc. Von Rad also links cyclic time with cyclic myths corresponding to the natural cycle, but this has been called a later rationalization.[54] These confusions are exemplified in his comparison of Western and Israelite views of time. This passage (II.99ff.) defies clear analysis.[55] Western time is linear, absolute, abstract and eschatological. The first three attributes are sometimes contrasted and sometimes identified (II. 99f.) whilst the fourth is contrasted with the Greek cyclic view of time, which is itself a disputed view.[56] Anyway, von Rad really means that history, not time, is eschatological. Further, I doubt whether von Rad has characterized the Western view of time correctly, since it is doubtful whether we think of 'time without events' which is *one* of the meanings given for 'absolute time'.[57] One reason for this lack of clarity is the confusion when spatial metaphors are applied to time, and another is that there is no single Western idea.[58] In some ways we think of time as cyclic, repeating itself every twelve or twenty-four hours or every year. At the same time we think of time 'flowing', recognizing that some events recur and others do not.

To this confused analysis of Western time he adds further confusion when he describes the Israelite view. Not only is this defined in contrast to Western time, but there are three Israelite views and the relation of these to each other is also confused. There is a general view (II. 99f.) which is presumably always applicable. There is an early Israelite view (II. 102), and a later view, the specifically Israelite view, although this is now a matter of history and not time (II. 105ff.). Even within sections there is confusion; absolute time is 'time independent of events' but 'in addition to' this there is 'abstract time', i.e. 'time divorced from specific events' (II. 99f.)!

Much of the evidence cited by von Rad does not seem to justify his conclusions. The failure of the Deuteronomic historian to enter the reigns of the monarchs of Israel and Judah on a single time span (II. 99f.) may be nothing to do with time but rather a way of interweaving the two histories as the history of 'Israel', i.e. God's people. Certainly statements like 'In the seventh year of Jehu, Jehoash began to reign' (II Kings 13.10) imply that although the streams of events were distinct, the time in which the events took place was not. How von Rad can claim 'Hebrew completely lacks a word for our modern concept of time' and use that to establish that she was not capable of thinking of time divorced from specific events, I do not know. If he means that certain aspects of our word 'time' had no Hebrew equivalent it may be true, but it would also be true for 'history' and *Heilsgeschichte*, but von Rad would hardly wish to deduce from that that she did not think about them. If he means that no Hebrew word covers the same semantic field as *Zeit* (time) that should surprise no one, but it is hardly significant. If he means that we can never translate any Hebrew words by our word 'time' he is wrong, for he does so himself. Von Rad comes close to identifying time and event for Israel, a view which is firmly rejected by J. R. Wilch in his detailed study of '*ēth*.[59]

Von Rad tells us that ancient Israel's view of time is typified by Gen. 8.22. 'The only way of conveying the idea that the earth will remain in being for ever is to construct a series of times having various contents' (II. 102). Presumably this shows that time could not be thought of without events. But this verse is not concerned with the nature of time but with assuring us of the continuity of the natural order. We are also told that this verse is also 'non-eschatological'.[60] But the passage presupposes that some events, e.g. the Flood, are once-for-all events. Certainly, for the Yahwist, time/history is moving to a fulfilment. The point is that history can be eschatological whilst nature is constant and time continues, which is basically our own view. True, the series of events follows the rhythm of nature (II. 102) but this does not mean that time or history is cyclic, rather it corresponds to reality. We must also remember that for the Yahwist this rhythm was ordained by God as much as any historical act. If this passage is typical of early Israel's views, then we must doubt whether von Rad has understood them properly.

It is the later view of history/time which is most important to von Rad, because it is this which he claims was unique. He sketches how Israel historicized her festivals (II. 104), thus freeing herself from the cyclic view, then made the events on which the festivals were based into a 'series of consecutive data' (II. 105) and finally broke through to a 'linear historical span' (*einer linearen Geschichtsstrecke*) (II. 106) by which is meant a linear time span. Thus there appears to be at least two Israelite views, one which contrasts with the Western view and one which has the similarity of being linear. If von Rad had been careful to differentiate between the various attributes of Western time, we could perhaps see how this later Israelite view was distinct from ours, but this he failed to do (cf. II. 107).

If I were to guess at what von Rad really means I would say we must distinguish three basic views of time.

(i) The early Israelite view which was similar to that of the ancient Near East, in which each event had its own time but in which there was no chronological connection envisaged between these time/event elements. There are only points of time identified by and identical with their respective events.

(ii) A later Israelite view, which developed out of the cult but was ultimately incompatible with it, in which certain of these time/event elements were grouped into a fixed order, so that a number of sequences of events emerged. On any sequence the events were fixed, although each chronological sequence was distinct from any other sequence, even if we would consider they had taken place simultaneously.

(iii) The Western view, where these chronological sequences are all integrated, so that not only are events on any sequence fixed in relationship to other events in their own sequence but also in relationship to events in other sequences.[61]

If this does represent von Rad's position it is unacceptable as a discussion of Israel's views of *time* and it is not supported by the biblical material, although it may have some value as a guide to the way she understood and presented *history*, since it is more a matter of causality than time. But it must be remembered that this view of history, is not unique and at the best is only a rough guide and generalization.

We must conclude that von Rad's discussion of time is hopelessly confused and much of it does not seem justified. This discussion is 'pivotal' and therefore confusion here is a very serious matter. On it is based von Rad's views of *Heilsgeschichte* and the prophets. So not only is the uniqueness of the *Heilsgeschichte* doubtful, but also the description of Israel's views of time, on which it is based, are unacceptable.

(c) The problem of Heilsgeschichte, *history and modern historiography*
In 1874 Oehler maintained that it was the task of an OT Theology 'to exhibit the history (sc. of Israel) as Israel believed it'. This was the case even for those who unlike himself did not accept 'that the thing believed was also a thing which took place'.[62] Von Rad's *Theology* is perhaps the first to be written under this specific tension. He was concerned with Israel's history 'without admixture of modern views'[63] but also accepted a picture of Israel's history constructed by modern historico-critical research which diverged enormously from the biblical picture. He was quickly

accused of emptying the *Heilsgeschichte* of any historical basis. Yet, one of his reasons for basing his *Theology* on the *Heilsgeschichte* and not the 'world of faith' was that he believed Israel's theology was about history and was not an ideology or mythology. Only by concentrating on the *Heilsgeschichte* could he hope to gain a real hearing for what Israel had to say about history.

Von Rad's position was not altogether clear in 1957 (when I was published) but he has clarified and modified his position in response to criticisms which have been made. In I he acknowledged clearly the problem caused by the chasm between the two pictures of Israel's history: 'This raises a difficult historical problem' (I. 106, cf. I. 108). He also implied that the historico-critical picture was the truly historical one, for it is a 'picture of the history as it really was in Israel' (I. 107) and it seeks for a 'critically assured minimum' (I. 108). In contrast, the OT's picture is personal, confessional and 'tends towards a theological maximum' (I. 108). Faced with this discrepancy, von Rad said that 'for the present, we must reconcile ourselves to both of them' (I. 107), but when engaged in constructing an OT Theology he is concerned with Israel's picture, the *Heilsgeschichte*. In dealing with that, 'we are not . . . concerned with the philosophical presuppositions' of historical research (I. 108). Granted von Rad's premises this position might seem clear, but criticisms have revealed much which is ambiguous.

The apparent denial of any connection between the *Heilsgeschichte* and history caused Eichrodt to write with fury, condemning von Rad as an existentialist (I. 514), a title which he does not deserve.[64] But since then, von Rad has many times asserted that he did not wish to deny that the *Heilsgeschichte* is firmly rooted in history. Even early Israel was 'obsessed by its actual history' (II. 424).

The kerygmatic picture too (and this even at points where it diverges so widely from our historical picture) is founded in the actual history and has not been invented (I. 108).

Eichrodt's criticism was not aimed solely at von Rad's methodological comments but also at the two pictures of Israel's history presented within the *Theology*. These were so divergent that it seemed impossible to restore 'any inner coherence' (I. 512). Later von Rad said, 'We are convinced in the last analysis of a connection, indeed a unity, between the two viewpoints.'[65] This however, seems to be a change of view from that expressed in 1957, that the faith of Israel was unrelated to 'the results of modern critical historical scholarship' (I. 106).

This issue was clarified in von Rad's discussions with Hesse, Hempel, Maag and Conzelmann,[66] where he insisted that what really happened and the historico-critical reconstruction are not synonymous. This was his reply to the criticism that he was basing theology on events which did not happen.

Three other types of criticism about *Heilsgeschichte*, history and historiography are relevant here. J. A. Soggin challenged von Rad over the size of the discrepancy between the two pictures of Israel's history.[67] He placed the problem in its own historical context, thus showing that it arose at a time when the historian was more confident than to-day about the certainty of his picture. Inevitably new methods and materials have led to modifications. In particular, American historians have necessitated modifications to the Germanic picture on which von Rad's views were based. Further, von Rad's generalizations about Israel's view of her history were misleading: it was not developed completely by faith, nor was it only 'confessional and personally involved to the point of fervour'. The main thrust of these criticisms is that von Rad's generalizations hide important differences in the OT material, where history, chronicle and saga are all to be found. This point has been amplified by J. Barr:

> The Bible has no linguistic term corresponding to 'history' . . . its narrative passages are not constant but variable in their relation to what we, by any definition . . . can call history. . . . The relation which the OT stories bear to history varies in relation to a number of variables. These variables include the chronological remoteness of the events being described, the nature of the events . . . and the stage of historiographic technique at the time of writing.[68]

To all this a further variable must be added. As Vriezen points out, Israel did not have a *uniform* view of her own history, indeed sometimes her pictures are conflicting.[69] Thus, von Rad's generalizations seem somewhat rash.

Von Rad's generalizations about scientific history writing can also be criticized. Vriezen takes his comments about a 'critically assured minimum' to refer to the material on which the picture is constructed.[70] He insists correctly that scientific history must take some account of all the available material. However, I think that von Rad meant that critical history would only assert that for which it had very good evidence, it will not go beyond that which it can establish. Nevertheless, history has the responsibility of giving a plausible explanation of a stream of events and if evidence is not available a probable hypothesis may still be suggested. I am not therefore sure that all critical history can be content with this 'critically assured minimum'.

Alongside Soggin we can place E. Rust, J. Bright and G. E. Wright who all insist that the *Heilsgeschichte* does not have to forfeit its historical anchorage.[71] They all, in a variety of ways, find that rather than reconciling ourselves to the inevitable discrepancy of the two pictures, we should see that they are in fact reconcilable. And as we have been, von Rad appears to have now come to a similar position – at least in theory.

In practice too, it seems that von Rad is more committed to the historicity of the *Heilsgeschichte* than he had originally realized. When Hesse criticized him he tried to refute Hesse by choosing the Fall of Jerusalem to show that his Theology was not based on events which did not happen. Of course, the historicity of this is not usually questioned.[72] Again, von Rad is forced to integrate the two pictures: only so could he claim that Jonah 'should not be read as an historical account' (II. 289), or criticize the Chronicler's presentation of history (I. 351ff.).

A consideration of the above discussion surely raises the question whether Israel herself thought of all the *Heilsgeschichte* as having the same sort of relationship to the past, i.e., to what happened. We would suggest that von Rad's total separation of the two pictures would only be justified, if at all, if it could be shown that Israel was uninterested in the historicity of the saving history. Although she did not use the methods of historical criticism she was probably concerned with the historicity of events, and this concern is met for us, however inadequately, by this method.[73]

The second type of criticism concerns the different methods on which the two pictures are based. Von Rad argued that the critical history allowed no room for the operation of God which was the special concern of Israel's view of history. This he said should not be dismissed lightly as 'unhistorical', as Hesse appeared to do. C. Barth criticized von Rad for accepting the premises of positivistic historiography. The premises of E. Troeltsch, with the consequent rejection of all superhuman causality as non-historical, 'may have been binding on the historical critic for a long time but they do not have to remain for ever'.[74] Really, this appears similar to von Rad's own position. For, he implies that if the historian refuses, on methodological grounds, to say anything about God's relation to history, then he forfeits the right to say that he alone can deal properly with the past. However, whilst von Rad is in danger of antagonizing the historian and of emptying the *Heilsgeschichte* of any historically verified events, Barth's suggestion would lead to co-operation.

The third type of criticism comes from R. Rendtorff.[75] For him the traditions and history, i.e. what really happened, cannot be separated. Israel's real history is only accessible to us through her traditions, and these made a vital contribution to her actual history. The *überlieferungsgeschichtlich* method, used by von Rad, must push beyond the traditions to the events which gave rise to them as well as follow the development of the traditions. History cannot be restricted to political events and therefore the traditions are part of history. When Rendtorff and others claim that both parts of his *Theology* are dependent on the historico-critical method, and therefore when he deals with the *Heilsgeschichte* he is still dealing with the historico-critical method (contra I. 106), they do him less than justice. The real point is that the two pictures of Israel's history are the product of very different intellectual activities (I. 106). Certainly we *construct* the historico-critical picture of Israel's history by the same method as we *reconstruct* Israel's picture, but originally Israel *constructed* this picture in a different way and for a different purpose. Even so, this does not entirely exempt von Rad. If, as he maintains, the historico-critical picture is not relevant theologically because it was a picture with which Israel had nothing to do (cf. I. 106), the same must be said of the historico-critical reconstruction of the *Heilsgeschichte*. For Isaiah had no more to do with von Rad's account of traditions than with the historian's picture of Israel's history; both were seen through his own non-historico-critical eyes.

If Rendtorff is right to argue that Israel's traditions influenced and were part of Israel's history, as I believe he is, this would also be true for Israel's 'world of faith', so again the absolute distinction which von Rad maintains would disintegrate. In one respect, Rendtorff has not allowed historical criticism sufficient scope, for, it will ask whether Israel's interpretation of the original event was justified.[76] So the recognition that traditions are part of history does not solve all the problems.

So far, the criticisms we have considered have been concerned with the *Geschichte* part of *Heilsgeschichte*. Other critics attacked von Rad's concept of *Heil*. Both Hesse and Baumgärtel insist that theologically von Rad must start from the NT view of *Heil*.[77] Hesse believes that the NT insists that it was in the real history that God was leading on to the coming of Christ, and not in the misleading descriptions of that history preserved by Israel.[78] Von Rad asserted that the historian refused to say anything about God in his picture of Israel's history, so he could not see how that could be theologically relevant.[79] In doing this, von Rad was oversimplifying Hesse's position, for he included in that real history the faith of each biblical witness – hence, the stories of Abraham are valid not as a testimony to the historical Abraham but about the faith of the narrator.[80] Once again the 'world of faith' would become integrated with the *Heilsgeschichte*. Against Hesse, it must be questioned whether the NT does guarantee that it is the real history which is theologically relevant, because most probably the NT accepted the OT's picture uncritically. Von Rad is therefore right to see that we *have to* distinguish them. Against both Hesse and Baumgärtel von Rad can argue that our concept of *Heil* should not be restricted to the NT concept in isolation from the OT. The NT does not see a totally different religion in the OT since it considers itself addressed directly by the OT traditions and appropriates them in the same way as the OT did. Further, von Rad believes that both Testaments reveal God acting in history for men's salvation. Much of Hesse's and Baumgärtel's criticisms of von Rad's concept of *Heil* seems unjustified.

Let us now try and clarify von Rad's position and draw together criticisms which remain unanswered. Von Rad recognized that the two pictures are reconstructed by us by the same method; his point was that Israel had a different method and aim. In separating the two pictures he wanted to underline the different epistemological uses: 'We must consider whether we have not too naïvely combined the OT's way of thinking about history with our own . . .' (I.417, cf. II.424). Although modern historiography denies any acts of God, Israel's concentration on this aspect of history may help us to overcome our inability to trace God's work in history and so to see a little more of the incredibly complex phenomenon of history. Israel's view 'carries with it its own justification, stature and law' (I. 117),[81] even though the scientific method is most appropriate for matters of cause and effect.

Even this position is not without difficulties, although von Rad seems largely unaware of them. If we do not evaluate the historicity of the OT's picture of the history by comparing it with the historico-critical picture, by what can we evaluate it? If we accept that it was not the intention of the OT to present a critical picture of history, how do we know that it really wanted to write *history* at all? Can we just *accept* that what is expressed was 'Israel's definite historical experience of Yahweh' (II. 421) and that the kerygmatic picture 'has not been invented' (I. 108)? Even if we accept that it arose out of some experiences of some of the people, what of all the other experiences which were not so expressed? Were the right experiences chosen? Was God not at work in others? We could ask other questions on these lines.

Secondly, von Rad believed that however much Israel's picture diverges from that of the historian, it too is grounded in real events. Von Rad would never say of the *Heilsgeschichte* that it has 'spurious factuality' (Eichrodt I. 513). The reason for the confusion is that the events described in the biblical picture (the referent) need not be the events which gave rise to the picture and which ensured its contact with history (the source). An account of the Exodus might reflect Israel's experiences with God in the tenth century, so that the events to which Israel's faith is related need not be the events described.[82] But, because it expresses an historical experience, it is *Heilsgeschichte* and not mythology.

Only rarely does von Rad attempt to answer whether the referent (which as a tradition would usually be an amalgam of referents and sources) or the source was more influential (cf. II. 421). All this raises the question whether his *Theology* would not have been more helpful and accurate if it had concentrated on the events to which the faith was related and not the referents, i.e. the *Heilsgeschichte*. Again, this would have led to a break down of the dichotomy of 'world of faith' and saving history, but time and time again we have seen this is indefensible. Certainly, it would have helped von Rad to circumvent the schizophrenic position of rejecting the historico-critical picture and still using it, for instance, to interpret the Deuteronomic history (I. 342).

Thirdly, and this is an issue which von Rad does not appear to have clarified, is the *Heilsgeschichte* to be valued theologically as a testimony to certain primary events (the events of the *Heilsgeschichte*) or to the events which Israel actually experienced, or as a narrative portrayal of the meaning or nature of history?

Obviously von Rad's position contained many ambiguities and problems of which he was not fully aware in 1957. Equally, the fierceness of the criticisms he engendered suggests that his brave separation of the historico-critical picture and Israel's picture of her history focused attention on an important problem. I personally doubt whether von Rad has succeeded, any more than Eichrodt, in drawing attention to history as the place of God's activity and revelation. Certainly, we have frequently had to indicate that the total separation of *Heilsgeschichte* and 'world of faith' is unacceptable. Von Rad has not succeeded either in overcoming the separation to which he pointed, although the criticisms of some (e.g. Soggin, Barth and Rendtorff) have indicated lines of progress, or in keeping the two methods and the two pictures apart. When to this we add the fact that von Rad's reconstruction of the *Heilsgeschichte* would be unrecognizable to anyone in Israel, the justification for his *Theology*, and in particular the absolute separation of the two pictures of Israel's history, seems slight.

(d) Heilsgeschichte *and the prophets*
Von Rad maintains that an OT Theology can be evaluated by the way it integrates and expounds the prophetic message: 'The most accurate test of the starting-point and arrangement of a theology of the OT is . . . the phenomenon of prophecy' (I. 128). It is rather unfortunate for his *Theology*, then, that it is inadequate here.

In the first place, he is involved in an apparent contradiction concerning the relationship between prophecy and saving history. We are told, 'The prophetic message is specifically rooted in the saving history' (II. 303). Only so could von Rad expound the prophetic message appropriately within a *heilsgeschichtlich* Theology. Accordingly, he had argued earlier that there was no fundamental theological distinction to be made between prophetic predictions and the witnesses to past history.[83] It is understandable then, when he says, 'Our particular concern has been to put the prophets back into the saving history and to pay heed to the aspects of prophecy which results from this' (II. 298). In contrast, he is equally insistent that the prophets and the saving history do not go together. The prophetic conviction 'places them basically outside the saving history as it had been understood up to then by Israel' (I. 128). Indeed, it is for this reason that his *Theology* had to appear in two separate volumes, 'within the scope of a theology of the historical traditions there can be no mention of the prophets' (I. vii).[84]

In commenting on this contradiction, C. A. Keller says that the prophets 'are entangled in an insoluble paradox in that they affirm the *Heilsgeschichte* and yet deny it'. This inconsistency is not actually to be found in the prophets, but it is created, Keller adds, by von Rad's 'fundamental concept' of *Heilsgeschichte*. Von Rad did not distinguish between the fact of the *Heilsgeschichte* and the false security which the Israelites had on its basis.[85] Von Rad could avoid Keller's criticism if he accepted that there was an objective *Heilsgeschichte* (not necessarily the course of history reconstructed by the modern historian but the true history of God's relation with Israel) and also a subjective *Heilsgeschichte*, i.e., what Israel believed this history to be. His phrase 'as it had been understood up to then by Israel' suggests that it was this subjective *Heilsgeschichte* from which the prophets must be separated. Further, as he places each prophet in his correct historical position and locates the traditions which the prophet uses, it seems that von Rad attempts to put them back into this objective *Heilsgeschichte*. However, if this solution helps to solve the 'paradox', it creates another problem, for if von Rad admits that this objective salvation history is distinct from Israel's view, then in expounding Israel's traditions he cannot claim to be expounding the real *Heilsgeschichte* at all. Thus, the theological validity of his work would be even more in doubt.

The contradiction over the relation of the prophets to the *Heilsgeschichte* is not the only difficulty in von Rad's position. The absolute separation of prophetic and historical traditions cannot be accepted, since the two traditions are linked both historically and biblically.[86] Zimmerli is quite correct to question whether it is legitimate to treat the Priestly tradition as though there had been no prophets.[87] Von Rad himself admits that 'E' was probably from northern prophetic circles and that Deuteronomy was influenced by prophecy.[88] Conversely, it is part of von Rad's case that the prophets were influenced by the historical traditions.[89] Even here Fohrer is correct to point out that von Rad has not considered carefully enough whether the prophetic message was received through the historical traditions or was merely expressed in terms of them for the convenience of the hearers.[90] Again, von Rad used much prophetic material in I and much historical material in II.[91] Further, von Rad has suggested that the real break is not between prophecy and historical traditions but within prophecy.[92] He says that it is only with Jeremiah, Ezekiel and especially Deutero-Isaiah that the breach with saving history is emphasized (I. 127). Yet, even here, 'it would be wrong to speak of a complete breach in the saving history' (II. 272).[93] It seems that von Rad really just wanted to expound each prophetic message and so tried to rule out the alternative ways of treating them by appeal to *Heilsgeschichte* (cf. I. 128). This has resulted in the usual contradictions and ambivalence.

A third problem concerns von Rad's reason for wishing to put the prophets back into the saving history. This becomes clear when he discusses the danger of a systematic treatment of the prophets. He utters a warning that such a treatment must 'in no case obscure their position in the saving history. . . . The message of each prophet was exactly directed to meet a specific time' (II. 299). Here again, it looks as though von Rad means the 'objective' saving history. It would appear that a similar claim could be made for the historical traditions which were also written for specific situations. In their case, however, von Rad is forced to admit that it was impossible to give 'a history of the credal statements of Israel in chronological sequence' (I. vi) because the traditions cannot be given sufficiently precise geographical and historical locations. Thus, he is forced to settled for the subjective saving history order, 'those contexts in the saving in which it was arranged by Israel' (I. vi). It would seem therefore that the two parts of his *Theology* are essentially different. The second point to note in connection with this issue is that, whilst his claims for the prophets need not be disputed, an important rider must be added; the prophetic message was reinterpreted and reapplied from the time the oracles were collected until Qumran. So the prophetic message was not considered to be *only* directed to a specific time, it was a living word of continuing relevance.

We are forced to conclude that if an OT Theology is to be judged by the way it deals with prophecy in relationship to the other parts of the OT (cf. I. 128), von Rad's *Theology* is not to be highly commended. Eichrodt's method allows him to bring out the 'bewildering dynamic effect' of prophecy with equal clarity and greater comprehensiveness. Of course, this does not mean that von Rad's exposition of the prophets is not to be highly commended. He has brought fresh exegetical insight and stimulation to the study of the prophets – but it is as a book on prophecy and not as an integral part of an OT Theology that it has value.[94]

Von Rad's use of *Heilsgeschichte* to deal with prophecy in relationship to his *Theology* is not acceptable, any more than it is for the other topics we have considered.

(e) Heilsgeschichte *and the NT*

Although we shall consider von Rad's treatment of the relationship between the two Testaments more fully in the next chapter, we can indicate here that *Heilsgeschichte* is again of crucial importance. Von Rad insists that a proper appreciation of the relationship between the two Testaments is essential for his work:

> Only when OT theology takes the final step to the threshold of the NT . . . and when it is able to make men believe that the two Testaments belong together, will it have the right to term itself a theological undertaking (II. 428f.).

He also insists that the proper relationship between the Testaments is a saving history one.

> The chief consideration in the correspondence between the two Testaments does not lie primarily in the field of religious terminology but in that of saving history . . . (II. 382).

Again, he stakes the theological validity of his OT *Theology* on *Heilsgeschichte*. Once again we shall be forced to conclude that this pre-eminence is not justified.[95]

Conclusions

We have drawn attention to the importance of *Heilsgeschichte* and the claims von Rad makes for it in relationship both to the OT and his own *Theology*. His *Theology* stands or falls *as a Theology* with the validity of these claims. Our examination has shown that not only is there much conceptual confusion over the term but also that the major functions attributed to it by von Rad cannot be justified. So most of von Rad's reasons for writing his *Theology* as he did cannot be accepted, although many of his exegetical insights will remain, for his practice is far better than his principles.

IV

COMPARATIVE ISSUES

We shall continue our examination of the two *Theologies* by investigating a number of issues which are of considerable importance for most contemporary OT Theologies and certainly for Eichrodt's and von Rad's.

1. *Old Testament Theology and the Old Testament*

We have seen that Eichrodt and von Rad differ considerably in their conceptions of the tasks, method, presentation and basic concepts of an OT Theology. Equally, we have seen that von Rad wished rigidly to distinguish his approach from that of an Eichrodtian type, but that he has not succeeded in justifying this. Further, although Eichrodt was extremely critical of von Rad's view of the relationship between history and revelation their attitudes to it were similar. How great then is the difference between the two Theologies once the superficial differences are removed? Do they in fact have a different understanding of the OT as well as of the nature of OT Theology? Or are they the same thing dressed differently?

It is possible to show that the proportions of material used from any one OT book are roughly the same in both Theologies, although Eichrodt uses the Psalms proportionately more than von Rad.[1] This means that in both *Theologies*, Genesis, Exodus, Deuteronomy, Psalms, Isaiah, Jeremiah, Ezekiel and Deutero-Isaiah are used often, whereas Ezra-Nehemiah, the Minor Prophets (other than Amos and Hosea) are seldom mentioned. It is clear that both find it difficult to use certain types of material, such as lists of names, tribal divisions, some cultic descriptions and secondary prophetic material. It seems that von Rad's different approach has not enabled him to use very different material from that used by Eichrodt. Eichrodt avoids oracles of Doom on the Nations, which do not agree with his own views of universalism, whereas von Rad plays down the theme of Restoration which does not fit well with his claim that the NT is the fulfilment of the OT promises.[2] But, to a large extent, the actual biblical basis of the two *Theologies* is similar. Of course, the distribution of the OT material differs. For instance, most of the references to the Pentateuch and Former Prophets occur in von Rad I, but they are spread more evenly through Eichrodt's two volumes. In Eichrodt's case, it is worth noting that the Writings, unlike the other major divisions of the Canon, are used far more in II than in I.[3]

In some ways von Rad's *Theology* appears to be the more biblical because he has a great propensity for quoting the OT, sometimes at considerable length. In the case of Deutero-Isaiah, where the Servant Songs are quoted in full, it may be because 'we cannot fully understand them' (II.250). Too much stress should not be placed on this tendency however, because he seems to have chosen the passages for their literary-poetic qualities more than their theological significance.[4] It has been suggested that Eichrodt prefers to paraphrase, rather than quote, because of his desire to get biblical ideas across to us which he does not think the biblical language itself will do. I would suggest that more important reasons are saving of space and his synthesizing approach, for a paraphrase can be made to cover a larger number of passages than an explicit quotation. This often results in a loss of precision.[5]

If we examine the ways that the OT material is used we can recognize similarities. For instance, both construct accounts of themes, such as covenant, righteousness, holiness, zeal, glory, angels, sacrifice, sin, atonement and the divine names. Although these themes are more numerous and extensive in Eichrodt's *Theology* they nevertheless have an important place in von Rad's. Similarly both give accounts of offices such as priests, Levites, judges, kings and prophets.[6] In most cases, von Rad starts his exposition on the basis of some strand of the OT for which the particular theme is important and juxtaposes other views on the same subject. In Eichrodt's they are discussed as they occur in *his* structure. Von Rad's method has the advantage of placing the theme in *an* OT context rather than one which he has constructed, but it also has disadvantages. When he does not develop themes in this way (e.g. the love of God in Deuteronomy, or faith in Gen. 15.6) we lose the mutual illumination of similar thoughts from other parts of the OT. When he does broaden the scope of his material, it holds up the running exposition and places the other material in an alien context. Anyway, the author's subjective judgment is still called for in deciding which strand of material the theme is most important for, and where it should therefore be developed. There are also certain themes which are not developed. Von Rad explains his reasons for some of these (I. 356) but it is difficult to see why the major festivals receive no theological exposition[7] unless it is because their view of history is not the *Heilsgeschichte* one he wishes to develop (cf. II. 102ff.) Eichrodt can be criticized for giving the impression that ideas are eternal and without historical roots, although he does usually contextualize his major discussions of themes.

If von Rad can incorporate themes, Eichrodt can include ex-positions of whole books or strands of material. Although he does not give a description of the thought of individual prophets, in some cases, such as Love in Hosea, or Holiness in Isaiah, we have compensation. Eichrodt's use of the Deuteronomic historian has been criticized by R. E. Clements, who says that its value for him is in its 'incidental allusions to the religious ideas of its leading characters'.[8] Yet Eichrodt too can use the 'word-theology' of the Deuteronomic historian (II. 73), and in general he can integrate the findings of 'Introductory' research, i.e., concerning questions of authorship, date, form criticism, etc., such as the Levitical preaching in Chronicles (II. 252) or the structure of Deuteronomy (I. 90ff.). He, as much as von Rad, expounds the primal history of the Yahwist (II. 401) and the book of Job (II. 517ff.). Certainly Eichrodt's discussions are briefer than von Rad's and they occur within thematic descriptions, but this is sometimes so for von Rad (e.g. his discussion of Job or the prophecies of the New Jerusalem). Once again, von Rad seems to me to be overstressing the difference between his own and previous Theologies, when he claims for his that it takes cognizance of 'the mutual intersection . . . during the last twenty or thirty years between introductory studies and Biblical theology' (I. v.)

Von Rad expounds the OT as bands of tradition and is not concerned primarily with the historicity of these traditions. After reading Eichrodt's vehement criticisms of this it is rather surprising to note that he too is often more concerned with expounding the material than with the historical reality behind it. This can be seen from his treatment of the Abrahamic material, angels, glory or name, etc. For instance, he shows no concern to establish or defend the historical nature of *kābōd* in P. Cultic objects, like the ark, occupy an intermediate position, for although he is concerned with their historicity he concentrates on their significance. Sometimes Eichrodt incorporates Israel's history of religion as an aspect of her theology (e.g. 'The Origin of the Monarchy', I. 438ff., 'The Degeneration of Nabism', I. 332f.). His presupposition is that the imprint of God can be seen in the total religious history rather than in her theology alone. But if von Rad can afford to concentrate on the traditions this is because he has already dealt with the historical referents in the 'History of Yahwism'. It is in their treatments of Moses that the two *Theologies* are opposed. Eichrodt treats him as an historical figure, synthesizing the various traditions as part of the total witness to the complexity and uniqueness of the founder of the religion.[9] With von Rad, Moses is treated entirely as a figure in tradition, whose historicity is minimal.

In spite of this basic disagreement we should not forget the essential similarity between the way the two *Theologies* present the OT material, neither should we think that the two *Theologies* add up to the same total, for they do cover different areas and are directed by different concepts. In von Rad's *Theology* there is nothing corresponding to Eichrodt's 'The Components of Human Nature' or 'The Effect of Piety on Conduct (OT Morality)'. Von Rad justifies his omission of the former by claiming it did not amount to much theologically (I. 356). But this could also be said of his own 'Israel's Wisdom deriving from Experience'. Eichrodt has nothing corresponding to 'The Praise of Israel' but von Rad neglects the 'Sacred Seasons'. Eichrodt also lacks 'The Oral Tradition of Prophecy' but its *direct* theological relevance is questionable. For the rest, in spite of different methods of presentation both cover a similar field of view and use the various types of OT material in the same proportions.

The next issue to consider is how far the differences in their *Theologies* can be accounted for by the differences in their critical standpoints, especially on source-criticism, dating, etc.[10] Certainly differences here do affect their *Theologies*, as can be seen from their

use of Job 28.28. Whilst Eichrodt interprets this as an integral part
of the poem of ch. 28, and the poem within the context of the book
as a whole (II. 88 n. 3), von Rad says it is 'most certainly of a later
date than the rest of the poem' (I. 447). Consequently, what is for
Eichrodt 'fierce polemic . . . against the presumptuous way in
which men fancy themselves to have sat in God's council . . .'
(II. 88), is for von Rad a 'crude twist'. Such a direct relationship
between the differences in their *Theologies* is rather unusual. Indeed,
their views are generally similar, as we shall now briefly indicate.

For the Pentateuch, both write of the Yahwist, Elohist, the
Priestly School and the Holiness Code. In the case of Genesis,
their source analysis is practically identical. It is true that Eichrodt
follows Smend's division of the Yahwist into J_1 and J_2 and von
Rad divides P into two strands, but in neither case does this
appear to affect significantly their *Theologies*. In fact Eichrodt's view
of the Yahwist is similar to von Rad's (cf. II. 243) and their views
of the nature of the Elohist source are also similar. With Deuteronomy, von Rad's critical opinion that 4.44–30.20 is a fundamental
unity is reflected in his *Theology*, for in his section on Deuteronomy
(I. 219–231), Deut. 1.1–4.43 is mentioned only once. Eichrodt does
not make such a distinction, although he accepts von Rad's
arguments for the influence on Deuteronomy of the festival for the
renewal of the Covenant (I. 123). Von Rad's *Theology* is more
tightly bound to his own view of the development of the Hexateuch, which may ultimately make his book more quickly archaic
and less acceptable.

Once more we find a large measure of agreement in their views
of the prophets. There is some divergence over which material is
secondary, but Eichrodt classifies as secondary material only four
passages which von Rad implies are primary, while von Rad has
seven which Eichrodt thinks are primary.[11] It is possible to show
that Eichrodt is more conservative about Isa. 1–39 and von Rad
about Ezekiel.

It is notoriously difficult to date the Psalms and they therefore
provide malleable material for an OT Theology. In practice it
is not always necessary for dates to be given or implied so that it
is not easy to compare their opinions here. However, whilst it is
possible to show that for most of the psalms similar dates are presupposed, and that Pss. 18, 19, 20, 29, 46, 48, 56, 61, 68, 76, 84, 89
are placed earlier by von Rad than by Eichrodt, I can find no case

of the reverse. Both scholars recognize the cultic background to the Psalms,[12] but Eichrodt has a strong tendency to use them as evidence for personal piety.

With the Wisdom material there is more divergence. Both scholars separate the Elihu speeches from the rest of Job and von Rad also separates ch. 28. Conversely, Eichrodt thinks that chs. 38ff. are only loosely related to the main part of the book (II. 520 n. 1) but von Rad considers they are its climax (I. 416). Eichrodt implies that Ecclesiastes is an individual product from the Hellenistic period (II. 494) but von Rad abandons this idea (I. 445).

There is definitely a different evaluation of the Deuteronomic history. Eichrodt tends to subordinate this to Deuteronomy (II. 73, 252, 345) whilst von Rad considers it to be very important theologically. Eichrodt tends to use it as evidence for the monarchical period[13] and von Rad for the theological views of the narrator.

In neither *Theology* do textual emendations or references to the LXX play a significant part. Both are usually content to work with the normal critical text.

We may conclude this sketch of their views on matters normally dealt with in an *Introduction to the OT* by acknowledging that sometimes differences in their views have affected their *Theologies*. On the whole, however, there is agreement. Both try to avoid controversy in this field and only rarely do they state their positions. Since an OT Theology presupposes views on such critical matters, it would be helpful if Eichrodt's *Theology* were prefaced with a brief statement of his position and if the various sections of von Rad's included more explicit acknowledgment of his.

A third major issue of importance is their assessment of the OT, especially the limitations which they feel it imposes on them.

In general, both accept that we can gain a fairly clear understanding of the OT as a text. They are seldom troubled either by textual or linguistic problems, or by disputed exegesis. Eichrodt rarely has problems dating the material, which is an important feature for his developmental sections. This is understandable if we remember that in such sections only a relative dating is needed, and also that material which is difficult to date can either be used where he maintains that the views did not alter, or it can be slotted into Eichrodt's pattern where it fits logically. The danger in the latter case is obvious. Thus to some extent, vagueness about dating makes the material more adaptable for Eichrodt's use. Von Rad is more troubled with dating, especially for the different strands of the Hexateuch, and this leads him to his method of presentation (cf. I.vi).

Von Rad tries to indicate that there is a 'second order' problem for us in our attempt to understand the OT. The Hebrews were 'far less concerned with linguistic precision' (II.84), the language was more poetic than analytic (II.170, 257) which makes it difficult for us. Often we may be striving for greater precision than the Hebrews had attained (I.19). Part of the problem is on our side, for our categories and concepts may confuse clear understanding. Equally we are not yet able to understand fully the theological content of narratives (I.365) because they are 'uncommunicative in the matter of theology' (II.208, cf. I.109). Although both authors are aware of the preparatory problems which must be solved before we can claim to understand the text, neither is really worried about them.

Both recognize that the OT material is inadequate if we want to gain a complete picture of Israel's religion and faith. They agree that our knowledge of cultic traditions and the cult, especially for the early period, is greatly hampered by lack of adequate material (Eichrodt I.87, 128, 129, 141, 147 n.7, 161 n.6, 370, 393, 397, 398, 420; II.38, 225; von Rad I.12 n.21, 15, 16, 21, 29, 44 n.4, 77, 87, 186, 244, 249, 281 n.4, 282, 291, 363, 364, 405) and there are problems with prophecy (Eichrodt I.303, 320 n.3, 499; von Rad I.39f.; II.139, 147, 238). Yet although there is a similarity, it is the difference which is more significant. Von Rad seems more conscious of the problems, they appear to be constantly superimposed on his mind, whereas, once Eichrodt has been honest and mentioned them he gets on with his job as well as he can. Von Rad is especially doubtful whether we can gain any historical picture of Moses, and in general of that inner personal history of Israel's religion (cf. I.29, 37, 48, 57, 71, 84, 211; II.136). It may well be that it is this scepticism which caused him to write a different type of Theology, for obviously, an Eichrodtian type must have a certain confidence here. But on the other hand, von Rad can say,

It would be perfectly possible . . . to draw a tolerably complete and . . . a tolerably objective picture of the religion of . . . Israel, that is, of the special features in her conception of God, of the way in which Israel thought of God's relationship to the world, to the other nations and, not least, to herself (I. 105).

This seems to admit that Eichrodt's aim could be achieved. It is von Rad's emphasis on Form Criticism which enables him, or gives him the desire, to restrict any statement's validity to its *Sitz im Leben* and hence to narrow its field of reference. But von Rad should remember that not only was the OT created, it was also preserved, and it may therefore be valid evidence for the beliefs of the preserving groups as well as the originating ones.

From time to time positive evaluations of the absence of material are made. For instance, Eichrodt points out that in P there is no theory of the atonement, which shows 'that it is not within Man's power to set clearly defined limits to the effectiveness of sacrificial atonement' (II. 447). Similarly, von Rad considers it remarkable that Israel said so little about death, thus indicating her freedom from the bondage of mythology (I. 390). Such arguments are arguments from silence and before we can accept them as valid, we must be sure that no other explanation is possible, including the possibility that material has been lost (cf. von Rad I. 50).

A further limitation which both recognize is that the OT is non-systematic (Eichrodt I. 77, 111, 227, 283, 368, 464; II. 332, 409, 447; von Rad I. 116, 121). This recognition affects the *Theologies* in different ways. It leads von Rad to attempt to follow the OT's order as far as possible (I. 121) and Eichrodt to follow the OT's own 'dialectic', so he chooses covenant as his major concept (I. 33). Even so, von Rad thinks Eichrodt's type of Theology is too systematic (cf. von Rad I. vi, 111ff.; II. 410ff.): 'A world of religious concepts, later systematically arranged . . . never existed in Israel . . .' (I. 112). Probably Eichrodt would agree (cf. I. 69, 402, 406), but he would not accept that his *Theology* was therefore over-systematic.[14] Von Rad seems to be a 'naïve realist' in that he presumes his description of the OT is an exact and complete replica of it, a literal description of reality.[15] In fact, Isaiah's theology did not *exist* as von Rad describes it. The test of 'existence' is inappropriate; the real test is whether the description conveys *to us* an accurate account of the material being described. Von Rad has pointed out a much more important point when he admits that we are striving for greater clarity than the words allow (cf. I. 19).

Both scholars criticize the OT material at another level. They indicate what they consider to be limitations in the theological value of it. Eichrodt criticizes the *mālāk* concept because it is 'sound in sentiment but unclear in its mental images' (II. 29). On other occasions it is even more clearly the theology which is criticized. Eichrodt rejects traces of dynamism (II. 77, 82, 123, 186, etc.) and popular beliefs are criticized for their nationalism. He could justify such comments either from the OT's own presentation or from his view that God's revelation slowly purges out inadequate views (II. 324f.). Both Eichrodt and von Rad make critical comments about the later theology of Chronicles, post-exilic Judaism, scepticism and apocalyptic (Eichrodt II. 301, 308, 392, 421; von Rad I. 91, 349f., 453, 455; II. 303, 308). It is probably inevitable that the scholar's bias will show through, but every endeavour should be made to make clear the basis on which the judgment is made. Also the critical standpoint should not result in a failure to appreciate the views criticized. It is doubtful whether these conditions are met.

Conclusions

We must not overlook the great similarity of the biblical basis of the two *Theologies*, nor the fact that, in general, these two scholars share a similar critical position. Although Form Criticism has made a greater impact on von Rad's *Theology*, it has been taken into account by Eichrodt as well. Von Rad is more explicit about the limitations of the OT material, and this may be an additional reason why he restricted his task to 're-telling' the OT rather than attempting to construct a complete picture of Israel's faith. If so, it is worth recalling that to understand any part fully, we need to understand the whole to which it belongs. Both recognize the non-systematic nature of the OT, but this does not invalidate Eichrodt's approach, although more care is needed in not imposing our logic on the OT.

Although there are differences in their understanding of the OT, these differences are not as great as their differences in understanding of the nature of an OT Theology. It is very difficult to accept that it is von Rad's different view of the OT which is the major cause for his method of doing OT Theology, even though von Rad seems to think this is so.

2. *Old Testament Theology and the New Testament*

One of the characteristics of OT Theologies has been their concern to relate the OT to the NT, thus the issue is of crucial importance in our examination of Eichrodt's and von Rad's *Theologies*. Although they were written during a period when pleas that the OT has any special relationship with the NT, rather than with Judaism and Islam, were under suspicion,[16] both have insisted on this and indeed have staked the validity of their *Theologies* on their success or failure of dealing satisfactorily with it. Eichrodt says that the reason for writing his *Theology* was 'to make practicable the long obstructed path from the OT to the New' (I. 15), and von Rad claims,

Only when OT theology takes the final step to the threshold of the NT . . . and when it is able to make men believe that the two Testaments belong together, will it have the right to term itself a theological undertaking (II.428f.).

On the importance of this issue both are agreed. However, because their attempts to deal with it are integrally related to their *Theologies*, it is more illuminating to consider each separately.

(a) *Eichrodt*
We shall consider his position under three headings:
 (i) Theoretical comments; (ii) Prediction and fulfilment; (iii) Use of the NT within the *Theology*.

(i) *Theoretical comments*
The most important comments are found in his article on the subject in *ZAW* 1929, pp. 88f., I. 26ff., and 'Les Rapports du Nouveau et de l'Ancien Testaments'.[17] Nowhere has Eichrodt succeeded in stating his position with clarity. The central ambiguity which he has never really resolved is that of the precise epistemological status of the relation between the Testaments. Granted that Eichrodt believes there is a positive connection between the Testaments, the question of the status of this belief remains unanswered.

In his theoretical essay he maintained that as all historical research involved presuppositions, selection of material and goal concepts, it was legitimate, even from the historian's point of view, that an OT Theology be written to show how the lines of development within the OT reached their goal in the NT, and that historically the ground was being prepared for the revelation of Christ. But, if this is a presupposition of the historian/theologian, then if it is to be more than a belief, there must be ways of showing that it is more valid than the alternative beliefs such as that the OT is fulfilled in Judaism or Islam as much as Christianity. Eichrodt never dealt with this issue. He also complicates his position by granting to the OT theologian the right to use the NT because it is a vital reality for him and not merely a heuristic principle. It is true that Eichrodt realized that in doing this he would over-step the borders of scientific history, but he does not indicate how and where the line should be drawn.[18] He also overlooked the fact that not all theologians would accept a positive relation between the Testaments.[19]

His methodological comments (I. 26ff.) fail to clarify these problems, and make matters more complicated. He now mentions four levels of relatedness: (1) a 'bare historical connection'; (2) 'an essential characteristic'; (3) an 'historical movement from the OT to the New'; (4) 'a current of life flowing from the NT to the Old'. Presumably by 'essential characteristic' Eichrodt meant something over and above chronological and causal dependence. But if it is more, can it be manifested through the presentation of historical evidence, or is this the 'presupposition' by which he worked? If so, how can it be justified historically? Thus, it seems to me that he has not clarified the epistemological status of his belief that the two Testaments are positively related. I suspect that although he recognizes it is a 'presupposition' and not the conclusion of his research, he believes the presupposition is justified by the historical evidence, as he hopes his *Theology* will make clear.

If we return to more material issues, he tells us that this 'essential characteristic' which unites the two Testaments is 'the irruption of the Kingship of God into this world and its establishment here' (I. 26). This being so, it is somewhat strange that he organized his *Theology* around *covenant* and not *kingship*. This enigma is explained in 'Les Rapports', where we learn that covenant was the special manifestation of the kingdom of God in Israel. Kingship language had to be avoided in Israel because of its associations with pagan rulers, but anyway, 'the idea of *berīt* concurs with that of kingdom'.[20] So covenant preserves the flavour of the Old but integrates with the New. Kingship is the general category, manifest in Israel as covenant, in the world in general as a 'power of order and judgment', then revealed as itself in the NT. In choosing kingship as the mandatory concept for the NT, Eichrodt makes his *Theology* dependent on NT Theology as well as historical research. He seems much less aware of this than of his dependence on the historical method.

(ii) *Prediction and fulfilment*

Because Eichrodt believed that all that covenant stood for in Israel was consummated in the kingdom of God, it was important for him to be able to show that the NT was the fulfilment of the OT's predictions. Thus, although his treatment is brief (I. 501–511), it is structurally important. He says of the OT's hope of salvation that 'in this one issue are concentrated all the historical struggles to arrive at a right understanding of the divine revelation' (I. 490). Eichrodt rejected the old orthodox view, the spiritualizing approach, and the one which reduced the connection between the Testaments to one of hope (I. 502f.). He claimed it was the 'consummation of God's sovereignty' which was 'the inward essence and the outward ideal of OT prediction' (I. 504f.). Consequently, he is in danger of either considering only those hopes which can be reduced to this, or minimizing the differences within predictions, or ignoring the fact that Christ comes nearer to fulfilling some hopes than others. Whilst these hopes had to be expressed in the language of their times, this does not mean that they are all mutually compatible, even if allowance is made for their historical conditioning. These dangers are evident in his treatment.

Eichrodt considers the prophetic hopes to be the most adequate expression (cf. 'unchanging truth' I. 490). After the exile decline set in: the hopes became more nationalistic (I. 485, 489), more cultic (I. 486) and more encumbered with mythological imagery (I. 487); then, under Persian influence, transcendental dualism added confusion to confusion (I. 487f.). This picture is unacceptable. Having established that the hopes of the later period are confused he could imply that the prophetic hopes were pure and undefiled, the real thing, so to speak. Yet the comparison on which these claims were based is not fair. He compared *some* prophetic hopes with the *total picture* of the hopes of the post-exilic period. However, if he were to depict the great variety of prophetic hopes (including the threats of judgment on the nations) and add to these the popular hopes of the same time,[21] then the prophetic period *in toto* would appear as confused as that of the later period. Probably this distortion is unintentional, but it is the consequence of Eichrodt's presuppositions and of the nature of the material available.

The way that Jesus is supposed to have fulfilled the predictions is also unsatisfactory. Eichrodt claimed that the OT's hope had become so confused that it cried out for a 'critique and a reconstruction'. The unchanging truth needed to be set

in the very centre where it can dominate all else, while at the same time unifying its struggling contradictions . . . Both these needs are fully met in the NT confession of Jesus as the Messiah (I. 490).

Jesus fulfils the prophetic hope and so clarifies the confusion of the later period. However, even Eichrodt has to admit that Jesus did not do this. Only half the 'essential concerns' are fulfilled, since the universality of the new Creation, and [the] ending of the old world-order' (I. 508) are postponed for future fulfilment. So Eichrodt makes a virtue of this necessity by suggesting that this means that logical proof is ruled out, so making room for faith (I. 510)! What he fails to tell us is that this postponement was *one form* which the hope was taking in Judaism.[22] His claim that

the realization of salvation which Jesus offered presented a creative synthesis from a conglomeration of essentially divergent and organically unrelated components (I. 510)

must also be questioned. Not only is Jesus' synthesis only one of several contemporary attempts, but he certainly did not synthesize the 'conglomeration' depicted by Eichrodt, which included Philo's views.

Eichrodt's treatment of prediction and fulfilment, which is structurally so important, cannot be accepted. In the end he selected from the variety of OT hopes those which he believed Jesus came nearest to fulfilling, and by various dubious means he attempted to eliminate or minimize the importance of those views which did not fit in with this. To make matters worse, he used the 'confusion' of later views, which was really evidence for their variety, to emphasize the significance of Christ's fulfilment.

(iii) *Use of the NT within the* Theology

Because Eichrodt believes that the OT covenant is fulfilled by the proclamation of the kingdom of God in the NT he does not restrict his treatment of the relation between the Testaments to Christ's fulfilment of explicit hopes. Rather, he seeks to show that the whole OT, because it everywhere relates to the covenant, is also reaching forward to the NT's kingship. If the OT is not seen in connection with the NT, it has a 'torso-like' appearance. This is why many of his sections are linked to the NT. Eichrodt appears somewhat arbitrary in practice. The only chapters without such links are V and XIV/C. Both seem amenable to such links. In the case of wisdom, although it proved impossible to carry through rigorously the clear and logical critique of wisdom teaching (II. 89), if Eichrodt had followed his usual pattern, he could claim that the dilemma was solved in Christ, the Wisdom of God. In the former case, 'The Name of the Covenant God' could be linked with the NT use of Lord. There appears to be no rationale guiding Eichrodt in the smaller sections either. Sometimes, as with 'The fear of God' and 'The personal relationship with God in the post-exilic period' (II. 268ff., 301ff.) it appears that links are not made with the NT because these relationships were not continued in the NT. On the other hand, links can be envisaged for these, whilst Eichrodt stresses connections which would not normally be expected, as with the cultus. Arbitrariness in such an essential matter does not seem the best way to show the coherence of the two Testaments.

The nature of these connections also appears to be arbitrary. Sometimes, as with creation, the NT just took over the OT's beliefs (II. 117, cf. II. 450). Sometimes the NT perfects something which had already been adequately expressed: the holy place emphasized the historicity of revelation 'until the day in which the concrete historical fact of the revelation itself decreed its own independence of any holy place' (I. 107). Usually, Eichrodt is concerned to show that with the (post)-exilic period things began to go wrong with Israel's faith, because people tried to combine rationally the antitheses of revelation which could only properly be combined in the person of Christ and not by rational reflection.[23] Sometimes the NT restores OT beliefs which Judaism had lost, e.g. the delimitation between word and spirit (II. 79, cf. II. 44, 528). On the other hand, Eichrodt has to justify the NT's use of the concept of Satan which was not important in the OT before the post-exilic period (II. 208f.).[24] In practice, therefore, there is a very fluid relationship between the Testaments. The NT can clarify existing ideas, integrate ideas which appeared antithetical or which were synthesized unsatisfactorily in Judaism. Thus, for Eichrodt, Christ clarifies the given revelation, as well as fulfilling the hopes to which the OT pointed.

The greatest defect in Eichrodt's treatment is not so much the arbitrary manner in which he presents the relationship between the NT and the OT but the depreciative evaluation of the post-exilic period which is unfairly compared with the 'high-spots' of pre-exilic prophecy. Nevertheless, the arbitrary nature of his presentation weakens its potential for convincing anyone who is agnostic about the NT being the fulfilment of the OT. Its greatest asset is its flexibility: in theory, at least, there is room for objectivity.

(b) Von Rad

Von Rad's treatment of the relationship between the two Testaments is in II Part 3. The first three chapters were originally delivered as lectures and to this a fourth on Law in the OT has been added.[25] These chapters betray a lack of integration with the rest of the book and with one another. Indeed, they show an alarming confusion of thought, self-contradiction and ambiguity which makes it doubtful whether von Rad has amended the deficiencies he sees in other treatments (cf. II. 356, 388).

Chapter 3 D, which seeks to show that the Lutheran equation, OT = Law, NT = Gospel, is invalid, is quite convincing as far as it goes but it is not closely integrated with the rest. Rather, it appears to be an attempt to dispense with the very negative evaluations of the OT which are often found on the Continent. The main arguments occur in the first three chapters, but before we involve ourselves in the details it will be helpful to consider von Rad's understanding of typology, for this will make clear what the main issues are.[26] These chapters are, in fact, an expansion of von Rad's essay on typology.[27]

As usual von Rad is unhappy with the terminology he uses, because it has unfortunate overtones.[28] He wants to use it in a new way. He tells us that typology is a form of analogical thinking which sees certain significant similarities in apparently dissimilar situations. Once these similarities are perceived they provide mutual illumination. In general von Rad regards typology as 'an elementary function of all human . . . interpretation' but he is more concerned with the special form of typology which he finds in the Bible. He would distinguish this from poetic typology, which sees higher spiritual meanings in mundane matters, from mythical thinking which sees a correspondence between the heavenly realm and the earthly, from allegorical thinking which is bound to the letter of the text and lacks the historical sense of typology, and from modern historical study which is based on the principle of analogy which 'includes in principle the similarity of all historical events'. The special characteristics of biblical typology are that in contrast to myth it is concerned with correspondences in which both elements are unrepeatable and within the temporal order; in contrast to allegory it is bound to the historical sense;[29] in contrast to modern historiography it is an *heilsgeschichtlich* analogy. (Von Rad does not state this, but it is implicit; it is not that all events are analogous but that certain events are because they are part of God's plan.)

Von Rad distinguishes typology from allegory in terms of 'historical sense'.[30] This phrase has several possible meanings. It might mean that typology depends on real historically verifiable situations, persons and events, or it might mean it depends on a historico-critical understanding of the biblical texts. In fact, it can mean neither of these for von Rad, because, as von Rad repeatedly tells us, the historico-critical method was not available in biblical times. Indeed von Rad criticizes earlier uses of typology because they were concerned with objective correspondences (II. 371). For us, typology must restrict itself to the 'kerygma that is intended' and not be concerned with the details in which this is set forth.[31]

It is worth noting the motives which lead von Rad to a typological approach. He believes that this will enable us to deal with narratives, etc. as they are, thus avoiding the necessity of looking for some theological or spiritual meaning.[32] Hence we can pay proper attention to the *heilsgeschichtlich* nature of the OT. Secondly, he believes that this is the basic method used by the NT in its appropriation of the OT, and that form criticism shows that it is also the method used within the OT in the re-actualizations of old traditions, the whole process of which he summarizes as 'promise and fulfilment' (II. 369ff.). Thirdly, he believes that the NT was justified in its method (although not necessarily in the way it applied this) because there is a 'structural analogy' between the Testaments in that both are concerned with the interrelationship between the divine word and event (II. 363) for which the supreme analogy is the 'way in which men are confronted . . . with a God who continually retreats from them'. Thus, von Rad believes that typology is *the* appropriate method for understanding the OT in the light of the NT. Of course, he wants us first to understand the OT in the light of our methods for understanding the text, but then to go on from our understanding to look for a typological correspondence with the NT.

We will make some preliminary comments here, by considering Eichrodt's evaluations of all this. In his essay 'Is Typological Exegesis an Appropriate Method?', Eichrodt answers 'Yes' if typology is carefully defined and if it is recognized as *one* among many possible approaches.[33] He rightly objects to von Rad's position that he wants to make it the only valid method. In his assessment of von Rad's *Theology*, Eichrodt objects to typology because of its existential tendencies (I. 517). Although I doubt the validity of so describing von Rad, Eichrodt makes two interesting points. He objects because von Rad leaves the interpretation completely open; it is 'charismatic'.[34] Secondly he feels that in concentrating on the kerygma and denying objective correspondences von Rad robs the NT fulfilment of historicity. I think however that Eichrodt has misrepresented von Rad on the second point. Von Rad is not really concerned to deny the historicity of the kerygma or its fulfilment, but to protect typology from excesses of exegetical ingenuity. Nevertheless, as we have already indicated, and as we shall see later, there are problems about the relationship between typology and history.[35] James Barr has some pertinent comments on typology.[36] He correctly points out that the NT's use of the OT cannot be restricted to 'typology' and he is critical of the attempt to distinguish allegory and typology in terms of their relation to history. A further danger is that typology, even if, as von Rad seems to intend, it begins with the historico-critical understanding of the OT, may easily deny the original meaning any real significance.[37]

In an important sentence von Rad says,

This renewed recognition of types in the OT . . . is simply correspondent to the belief that the same God who revealed himself in Christ

has also left his footprints in the history of the OT covenant
people . . .[38]

But, besides raising the perennial question of 'which history', this
seems remarkably similar to Eichrodt's views on the basis of which
he provides a comprehensive picture of the similarity between the
faith of the OT and that of the New.[39]

We have now explained what von Rad appears to mean by
typology and how it integrates with his form-critical approach and
such concepts as *Heilsgeschichte* and the promise-fulfilment scheme.
With this in mind we shall now examine the three chapters in which
von Rad expanded his earlier views on typology and the relation
between the Testaments. In 3 A he surveys the NT's use of the OT
and offers some theological reflections on this. He concludes by
saying that the other chapters expand the statement that the 'foundations of Christianity rest on the Old and New Testaments together' (II.335). For *convenience*[40] (II.357) he deals separately with
the OT's ideas about the world and man (3 B) and then the saving
history (3 C) both of which he compares to those of the NT. So far
all may seem clear, but an examination of the content reveals this
is far from being the case.

When 3 B is dealing with the 'distinctive features in the OT's
understanding of the world' (II.338), of Man (II.347), and Death
(II.349), together with their relation 'to the message about Jesus
Christ contained in the New' (II.350), it is convincing. It gives an
objective description of Israel's views[41] which are compared with
those of the NT, arriving at the conclusion that 'These ideas as
they are expressed in the NT are no different in principle from
ideas . . . in ancient Israel' (II.350). Von Rad shows that the
religion(s) of which the OT and the NT are the literary expressions
are remarkably similar. Unfortunately, from von Rad's own
standpoint, the whole of this is irrelevant. He began this chapter
by saying,

All that was said in the last chapter shows the impossibility of defining
Christian interpretation of the OT by comparing the constitutive
characteristics of the religion of ancient Israel and those of the religion
of the early Church, both taken in isolation, and basing one's conclusions on the similarities and differences between them (II.336).[42]

Therefore, interspersed with his objective assessments there is
another approach to which von Rad feels himself committed,

because it was the approach of the NT itself. This approach is the charismatic re-actualization of OT passages in the light of Christ's coming:

The question is no longer to define the message of the old texts before the era of the NT, but to discover whether they still preserve their kerygmatic reality after Christ's coming (II. 336).

Indeed, it must be shown 'that it is only with the coming of Christ that the true actuality of these writings was revealed' (II. 336). It is not difficult to see that von Rad is utterly confused at this point. As a theologian he feels he must follow the NT's view, which does not deal with the objective meaning of the OT, to which he feels committed as a modern biblical scholar. We shall now illustrate this confusion and suggest the way out which von Rad should have taken.

He claims that a basic premise is that 'the OT can only be read as a book in which expectations keep mounting up to vast proportions' (II. 321, cf. II. 319, 389, 428). Sometimes, 'this does not answer the question whether it is also to be read as the book which foretells Jesus Christ' (II. 321), sometimes the OT never mentions or visualizes Jesus Christ (II. 319); again

The passages which interpret the various events which took place within the OT sometimes look away from their own standpoint in time and forward to Jesus Christ . . . (II. 382, cf. II. 333, 363).

On the other hand, von Rad goes to the other extreme of denying his basic premise: from Israel's point of view the forward-looking character of OT texts 'is not apparent' (II. 371).[43] Thus, von Rad does not know whether the OT does or does not look forward, nor whether or not it looks forward to Christ, nor whether it looks forward to Christ from within the OT or only from a Christian position.

Von Rad is in a similar dilemma when he discusses the interpretation of the OT. Although as an OT scholar he is committed to objective exegesis which is often not that of the NT's use of the OT, he strives to justify the NT's approach as well. He claims that there is a pre-Christian and a Christian interpretation. The former has come to light through our 'keener eye for history'; the latter alone was available for 'ancient exegesis', which took as its starting point the final meaning 'which the ancient words gained in Christ'

(II. 385). This Christian interpretation is to be accepted because it is charismatic. There can be no impartial proof (and hence disproof) of its validity (II. 333) although it is important to note that it only continues the process begun within the OT (II. 321). So, 'the way in which the OT was cited and interpreted and made to supply proofs was entirely proper'[44] (II. 332f.). It appears that von Rad would like us to accept both interpretations as equally valid. The matter cannot be left here. For, 'ancient exegesis' believed that the only proper interpretation of the OT (where it thought the OT related to Christ) was the Christian one. They were in fact prepared to contest that pre-Christian interpretations (i.e. those not related to Christ) were legitimate.[45] Von Rad cannot of course do this. In his dilemma we can see that again he is troubled by the problem of the 'two pictures' in another form.

Von Rad fails to explain what he means by 'entirely proper'. If it means 'successful and convincing' (II. 333) the question is 'convincing for whom?' It is surely because of our 'keener eye for history' that it can no longer convince us because we are aware of the legitimacy of the pre-Christian interpretations. When von Rad says that the only difference between the pre-Christian and the Christian interpretations is the 'starting-point' he implies that the pre-Christian interpretation can always be developed charismatically into a Christian one. But the question is not so simple. Because we accept the validity of a pre-Christian interpretation of Isa. 53, it may well be that our Christian interpretation of that passage would differ from that of the NT.

The ultimate enigma of von Rad's case is that if he were to establish it he would also disprove the theological value of his *Theology*, concerned as it is almost entirely with the pre-Christian interpretation of the OT. For, the logic of his argument is that ultimately it is the Christian, i.e. the NT's interpretation which matters.

In order to cut the Gordian knot we must begin by examining one of the many rash generalizations which von Rad makes in these chapters:

All these writings of ancient Israel . . . were seen by Jesus Christ, and certainly by the Apostles and the early Church, as a collection of predictions which pointed to him (II. 319).

Now, as the NT actualizes only a small part of the OT, there can be no proof that 'all' the writings were seen that way. Further, if von Rad is right to say that the Christian use of the OT must be selective,[46] then again this statement would be wrong. We must also note that there are OT predictions which Jesus did not attempt to fulfil,[47] while parts of the OT are quoted, not because they apply to Jesus but because they are permanently valid,[48] some parts of the OT are rejected by Jesus,[49] and some 'predictions' do not refer to Jesus but to other events.[50] Thus, even if we consider only the NT's use of the OT, von Rad is wrong. However, a more fundamental criticism must be made. All along von Rad seems to assume that to deal with the NT's use of the OT is the same as dealing with the relationship between the Testaments. This is not so. Not only have parts of the OT been actualized in the NT, the OT has been preserved *in toto*.[51] It is this which is of special interest for OT Theology. The issue which is relevant for an OT Theology, then, is not so much the way the NT uses the OT (cf. II. 335) but how and to what extent the OT (and the faith therein expressed) is related to the NT. It is here that von Rad's objective treatment of the similarities of the religion(s) of the two Testaments is so important. For it is this which indicates the theological value of his work. If it is established that there is a similarity, then the way in which the NT gave it expression is relatively unimportant for an OT Theology.

If we ask why von Rad does not see things this way, then *Heilsgeschichte* raises its ugly head again. He says of the NT's use of the OT, 'a law which determined the whole saving history of the OT comes once again into operation' (II. 332). It is for this reason that he concentrates on the promise-fulfilment pattern, which he observes in every NT reference to the OT.[52]

Von Rad uses *Heilsgeschichte* in two other ways to link the Testaments. The one which underlies his whole presentation is that of *Heilsgeschichte* as the sphere of revelation; an idea which is valid for both Testaments is 'that it is in history that God reveals the secret of his person' (II. 338). The second also helps to explain his particular treatment:

The chief consideration in the correspondence between the two Testaments does not lie primarily in the field of religious terminology, but in that of saving history, for in Jesus Christ we meet . . . with the same interconnexion between divine word and historical acts with which we are already so familiar in the OT (II. 382).

We notice, as we have often done before, that this qualified claim ('not primarily') contrasts both with a categorical claim made earlier, that we cannot recognize in the OT 'a thought world that is "very nearly that of the NT" ',[53] and a much less negative comment that if the OT provided appropriate concepts for describing Christ's coming 'this would be of far-reaching theological importance' (II.352). On this occasion *Heilsgeschichte* is made preeminent because the similarity of language is subordinated to history: 'when God began to reveal himself to her in history, he also gave her her language' (II.353).[54] Von Rad considers that it is not the language, or the concepts, which are fundamental, but that for which the language is appropriate, namely *Heilsgeschichte*. But this is not acceptable. Not only do 'different ways of speaking of the data of existence correspond to different apperceptions of them' (II.353), but different ways of speaking and thinking can lead to different apperceptions.

Anyway, von Rad's claim is unclear. Which Jesus Christ is it in which these 'interconnexions' are found? Is it the historical Jesus, the kerygmatic picture in those parts of the synoptics where Christ's actions are interpreted in the light of OT promises, or the Johannine Christ where signs and discourses are linked? Or is it the fact of the incarnation, that is, Jesus as a man, revealing himself by both words and deeds. Von Rad refers us to II.358. Here, however, there is such a variety of connections between word and deed that we just cannot tell what 'the same' might mean. More seriously, if the salvation history referred to is the one depicted by Israel, then the *Heilsgeschichte* connection becomes a matter of thought worlds anyway and not of objective reality. It seems to me that again von Rad makes far too much of the *Heilsgeschichte* and in so doing lands himself in a dilemma which can only be solved by relegating this to its proper place, as one link among others. Von Rad cannot solve the problem of the relationship between the Testaments in terms of *Heilsgeschichte*. The solution for von Rad's *Theology* is that, as he was able to show, there is a similarity of thought worlds, including that of the importance of history for revelation, and this similarity cannot be overlooked.

Conclusions
We have shown that both Eichrodt and von Rad are concerned with the relationship between the OT and the NT and that their treatments of this issue are related to their methods of presentation,

for Eichrodt's is integrated with his covenant theology and von Rad's with *Heilsgeschichte*. It has been necessary to be critical of both approaches. This does not mean that it is illegitimate to be concerned with the relationship between the Testaments, nor that it is impossible to show some significant positive links. I believe that Eichrodt is correct to refuse to limit the issue to that of the fulfilment of OT predictions and von Rad is certainly wrong if he intends to claim that every mention of the OT in the NT is an implicit claim that a promise is being fulfilled, or if he believes that the relationship between the Testaments can be reduced to this. We are not limited to seeing the OT through the eyes of the NT, even if our interest in and convictions about a relationship between the Testaments are ultimately kindled by the NT. What is appropriate for an OT Theology is to show if, where and how the God revealed in the one Testament is like the God revealed in the other. This may be a presupposition which will guide the OT theologian, but it must not lead him to falsify either the OT or the NT (if he comes to the conclusion that this presupposition is wrong, he must say so). Because predictions are important for both the OT and the NT, the question of the extent to which OT predictions and hopes are fulfilled will be an important aspect of the whole. Here, it will be important to bear in mind all that von Rad has shown us about the legitimate fulfilment of OT promises within the OT when we try to assess the validity or otherwise of claims that Christ fulfils OT promises. But we must not escape all critical decisions by claiming it is a purely 'charismatic' affair.

In spite of its faults, Eichrodt's treatment appears to me, more satisfactory than von Rad's, although a summary presentation of the main links, along the lines which von Rad incongruously takes, is in fact a more convincing method of presentation than scattered comments. Nevertheless, such a sketch would need to be undergirded with integrated comments such as Eichrodt provides. Of course, the relationship between the Testaments is linked to the three issues we are now to consider, namely the uniqueness, the unity, and the revelational content of the OT.

3. *Old Testament Theology and the Uniqueness of the Old Testament*

Eichrodt realizes that, in spite of all the many disagreements he has with von Rad, they both acknowledge that in certain respects

Israel's faith is unique,[55] when it is compared with the religions which surrounded her.[56] To a large extent they even agree about the content of this uniqueness. This can best be seen if we start from von Rad's summary of 'the distinctive features' of Israel's world view (II. 338ff.) and add to it references to the same points elsewhere in von Rad's *Theology* and in Eichrodt's.

(i) The world is created and is not an emanation of some deity, so the deity is not a natural power divinized (II. 339f., cf. I. 121ff.; Eichrodt I. 209, II. 98ff.).

(ii) Israel was barred from understanding the world in terms of myth (II. 340, 349, cf. I. 141; Eichrodt I. 41f., 231, II. 114f., 402, 497).

(iii) Sex was not divinized (II. 340, cf. I. 27; Eichrodt I. 121, 135, 148, 151f., etc.).

(iv) There was no place for cultic images (II. 339, cf. I. 214; Eichrodt I. 118, 215, contrast II. 391f.).

(v) Man is taken from the sphere of myth and therefore there is no place for magic (II. 349, cf. I. 34f.; Eichrodt II. 497).

(vi) Death was demythologized but was never appropriated by Yahweh (II. 349f., cf. I. 276, 389f.; Eichrodt II. 221f., 497, 500, contrast II. 496).

Both scholars mention other minor features, Eichrodt much more than von Rad. Eichrodt's additions include the understanding of communion sacrifice (I. 148), Deuteronomy's use of 'the Name' (I. 208) and features of God's personality such as his anger (I. 266, cf. 272ff.) and *ḥēsēd*. He also makes the claim that the total picture of God in the OT was unique (I. 286f.), that Israel had a unique understanding of human personality (I. 360) and ethics (II. 379f.). Israel's law has a distinctive flavour because it was always being modified by her belief in Yahweh's personal will. (I. 74, 76, 83, 90, 94, 96, etc.). Von Rad appears to agree here, as when he says:

How completely institutions were always subordinated to the sole personal will of Yahweh is made clear by the stamp which justice received in Israel (I. 94).

Thus, it can be seen that Eichrodt, whilst agreeing with much that von Rad considers to be unique, would go further in spelling out the details. Perhaps this is because the distinctiveness of Israel's religion was not so generally accepted when Eichrodt wrote his

Theology. It also helps to explain his methodology, according to which it was essential to compare the OT religion with the other ancient Near Eastern religions. Von Rad believed that the best way to understand the OT was to concentrate on the text rather than the *religionsgeschichtlich* context.[57] Hence, he may well have regarded more aspects of the OT as unique than he mentions explicitly.

Obviously, von Rad believed that Israel's view of history was unique,[58] and this Eichrodt also stated. Although, like von Rad, Eichrodt contrasted nature and history, [59] he did not make such a complete separation (II. 118, 254). For Eichrodt, the real contrast was between gods who were personified forces of nature and Yahweh who was lord of both nature and history. Yet, although Eichrodt mentioned that other deities were considered to have acted in history, he also claimed that in other religions 'it never occurred to them to identify the nerve of the historical process as the purposeful activity of God' (I. 41). This needs to be modified in the light of Albrektson's research. Albrektson showed that the gods were not always bound to nature and that the 'divine plan' for Israel was neither so clear nor so comprehensive as Eichrodt thought.[60] Yet Eichrodt's claims are more circumspect than von Rad's. Indeed Eichrodt anticipated Albrektson's conclusion when he claimed that the distinctiveness in Israel's idea of history lay in her idea of God (II. 115).[61]

The overstatement of the uniqueness of Israel's view of history shows that great care is necessary in making the comparisons. Neither von Rad nor Eichrodt is likely to fall into the danger of overlooking the distinctiveness of Israel's ideas or institutions which appear similar to those of the ancient Near East until they are placed in their proper Israelite context. But Mowinckel is correct to insist that 'each detail obtains its significance from the structure of the whole in which it has been incorporated'.[62] Eichrodt and von Rad run the opposite danger to the 'patternists' against whom Mowinckel was writing. For we need as sensitive an appreciation of the material with which we compare Israel's religion as of the religion itself. The errors about Israel's view of history arose partly because the individual aspects of other religions were not contextualized properly and therefore their real significance was not appreciated. It seems possible that Eichrodt would deny that other religions had this integration (cf. I. 517). Here, however, we must consider the warning of R. Benedict:

The case of cultural disorientation may well be less than appears at the present time. There is always the possibility that the description of the culture is disorientated rather than the culture itself.[63]

A third problem which unavoidably faces claims for the uniqueness of Israel's religion is that new material (or available material which has been overlooked) may show that apparently distinctive features are not really so at all. Thus, although Eichrodt's comparison of the P and Babylonian accounts of creation is cautious, it needs to be modified in some details in the light of recent discoveries.[64]

Nevertheless, apart from the criticisms we have made about their claims for Israel's view of history, much of their position seems well founded.

We have seen that both Eichrodt and von Rad recognize the importance of establishing that in some ways Israel's religion was unique, and that to a large extent they agree as to what features these are. Although neither of them is very specific about their reasons for this interest in the distinctiveness of Israel's faith, it is worth considering. It is partly to be explained as follows. Any objective account of Israel's religion must refer this to her religious environment, just as any valid account of her history will need the perspective of her political environment.[65] So, if one is going to relate Israel to her environment, then both similarities and dissimilarities must be indicated.

In both *Theologies*, however, another factor is operative. H. Gressmann raised the question as to how one could believe in Israel's election when in her inmost essence she belonged to the culture of the Near East. His answer was that if Israel was placed in this context, then, *like other nations* she had her 'individual soul with its specific qualifications and gifts' which would distinguish her from all others.[66] The similarity with Eichrodt's position is clear. He believes that Israel's covenant beliefs were unique and that they correspond to the revelation of a divine reality which is unique in the history of religion (I. 14). Thus, it is the uniqueness of her beliefs which evidence their revelational quality and this justified her claim to election (I. 369).[67]

There is however a problem. For, if Gressmann is right, Israel's uniqueness need be qualitatively no different from, say Babylon's religion.[68] Perhaps von Rad is half aware of this. He writes of 'an *entirely* unique understanding . . .' or of Israel as *'absolutely* unique . . .' and *'absolutely* without analogy . . .' and of 'her loneliness in the company of the religions of the world' (II.347, 349, 363, 340). At the same time he fears that from the standpoint of comparative religion Israel's literary legacy is 'a particular enigma *among the many* in the history of religion' (I. 321).

Although neither states it, they both need to establish the uniqueness of Israel's beliefs to strengthen the implicit claim that in some ways the OT is revelational. I am not sure that either fully realizes that they need to show that Israel's beliefs are unique in a way which is different from, say, the uniqueness of Babylonian beliefs. From the Christian point of view, the most legitimate way of doing this is to show that there is a special similarity between the OT and the NT. This may well be the unexpressed motive for their concern with the relation of the two Testaments. Of course, this would not *prove* that the OT should be given a special place, but it does seem a legitimate way of *supporting* the claim that the OT, as distinct from other religions, should be given revelatory status.

4. *Old Testament Theology and the Unity of the Old Testament*

A major disagreement between Eichrodt and von Rad, which has far-reaching implications for OT Theology, concerns the unity of the OT. It was part of Eichrodt's essential task to understand and make explicit the 'structural unity' of the OT (I. 31, 520), but for von Rad the unity of the OT is questionable and he thinks it improper to expect an OT Theology to deal with the question (II. 412, 427).[69] Both scholars are clear about the centrality of this issue and concerned about their disagreement (Eichrodt I. 517, von Rad II. 412f.)

To some extent, the issue is blurred by conceptual confusion. What exactly is, or should be, meant by the 'unity of the OT'? The existence of this confusion can be illustrated by their attitude to Köhler's *Theology*. Eichrodt associates von Rad with Köhler and contrasts himself with both, whilst von Rad links Köhler and Eichrodt and dissociates himself from both (Eichrodt I.518, von Rad II.412f.).[70] There are real differences as well, but in order to shed some light on this problem we shall begin by trying to make clear the concepts of unity used and the functions which, in Eichrodt's case, this concept has in his *Theology*.

When von Rad rejects the 'unity of the OT' he is equating unity
with systematic theology, i.e., it is some organized conceptual
unity, with no loose ends, no discrepancies and no contradictions
(II.412f., cf. I.111ff.). Such unity almost demands that it be the
work of a single mind. Hence it is not surprising that von Rad
denies there is such a unity in the OT. What von Rad does not
seem to realize is that Eichrodt also denies this. Even in his systematic presentation he is

not concerned with framing a system of religious concepts capable of
providing a complete all-round 'corpus of doctrine' in the form of a
consistent and harmonious intellectual structure (I.517, cf. I.14, 18,
II.21).[71]

A second view is that unity means what all the different ideas
have in common, the highest common factor. Von Rad is thinking
of this when he warns that 'we must keep an open mind toward
all the disparate and divergent elements . . .' (II.415). Now,
Eichrodt is occasionally concerned with this. He refers to 'common
basic features' (I.517, cf. I.210 n.1, 369, 482, II.96f.). We shall
suggest, however, that this is but one aspect of his understanding
of unity, and not very important. In view of von Rad's criticism it
is strange that he seems to decide that this is what he must look for.
In discussing the 'unity of the Bible' (which von Rad accepts) we
are to look for 'the typical element' (II.427).

A third possibility is that unity means uniformity. In rejecting
the unity of the OT von Rad says that Israel 'was positively at
pains to oppose the deep-rooted urge towards that unification of
concepts which is inherent in myth or ideology' (II.427). Certainly,
Eichrodt would deny that there was such a unity in the OT. He
insists that the proper place must be given to the historical nature
of revelation; that is why pre-critical orthodoxy must be rejected
(I.28). He himself recognizes much variety and even deals with
prophetic and priestly types of Yahwism separately.

A fourth concept is that unity means something complete in
itself. Although it is not easy to understand how von Rad can deny
the unity of the OT and insist categorically on the unity of the
Bible,[72] this does seem to be his reasoning. The OT is not a unity
because it is incomplete, all its promises demand the fulfilment
which comes with the NT, hence the Bible which includes the
promises and the fulfilment is complete and therefore a unity.

Again, Eichrodt agrees with von Rad that the OT is in some ways incomplete without the NT.[73]

What then does Eichrodt mean by 'unity'? Nowhere does he really define it, but his understanding presupposes that throughout the OT there is a testimony (with varying degrees of clarity) to the revelation of God at different times and in different places:

The one God yet reveals himself in different ways in the different periods of human history, and makes different claims on the obedience of his people (I. 284).[74]

With this understanding Eichrodt does not need to reduce everything to uniformity or concentrate solely on basic features. Rather, it is his concern to show how the tremendous variety of the OT reflects the same comprehensive reality from different angles. The variety in the OT is to be interpreted 'as the result of observing a complex reality from various angles' (I. 517). Conversely, individual views can only be understood accurately when they are related to the whole of which they are a part. The best name for Eichrodt's understanding is 'personal' unity, for its source is the personality of God. It can best be described as a series of disjunctives. First, it is a dynamic and not a static unity: the OT does not have to say the same thing everywhere, but from many different starting points it needs to be heading for one destination, even though the directness of the routes and the rates of progress vary. Thus, the different starting points in history and tradition are important for an OT Theology, as without them the goal will never be glimpsed. But the real interest is in 'the unchanging basic tendency of the message of the OT' (I. 13, cf. 402). Secondly, it is a personal and not a dogmatic unity. Hence, Eichrodt rejects attempts to present the OT as a 'corpus of doctrine' and welcomes conflicting trends which he explains as the result of the living nature of God (I.67, 104, 171, 205, II. 107, 456, 529). He emphasizes the unifying effect of the will of God on the newly formed nation (I. 39) on the development of law and morality (e.g. I.136, 209, 242), on the understanding of the world (II. 15, 96f., 112), on history (II. 356) and on individuals (II.498). It is because this will was first clearly expressed in the Mosaic covenant that Eichrodt gives such prominence to the covenant. Because Eichrodt allows for the historical conditioning of the revelation, his unity is one of central matters only and not of superficialities.[75]

It may well be felt that this concept of personal unity conflicts with Eichrodt's insistence on 'structural unity' and his interest in 'common basic elements'. By 'structural unity' he probably means the way in which the separate and sometimes apparently conflicting views unite in a structure which reflects the nature of the covenant God. The 'common basic elements 'are the links between ideas which, he believes, justify this integration. For Eichrodt, the unity which really matters is not some small part of the views held which can be abstracted from them all.[76] Rather, it is the larger whole of which the different views are just a part. This seems to me to be the correct interpretation of Eichrodt's position because it corresponds to his use of covenant. He does not mention unity very frequently, just because he thinks it is made clear by using covenant as his basic concept. It is important for his method because together with the uniqueness of the OT and the relation between the Testaments it helps to substantiate the claim that the OT should be considered revelational.

Having tried to clarify the various concepts of unity involved, we are now in a position to examine the debate between Eichrodt and von Rad and to assess the material differences between them. Straight away we see that they are not as diametrically opposed as they think they are. For von Rad too accepts that Yahweh provides a unifying factor: 'It can certainly be said that the object of Israel's faith was Yahweh and his action; but Yahweh and his purposes changed' (II.378).[77] 'Of course it can be said that Yahweh is the focal point of the OT' (II.415). Further, von Rad sees connections between the different types of Israel's religion. He insists that priestly and prophetic religion belong together. 'The faith of Israel cannot possibly be divided into two forms of religion. . . .'[78] (I.260, cf. II.328, 339f.) In calling the OT a history book (II.357) and in stressing that Israel always understood herself between a 'promise and fulfilment' (II.416, cf. 414) von Rad gives content to this unity.

Von Rad justifies his reluctance to concentrate on 'unity' by two 'arguments'. The first is in the form of a literary parallel. To expect an OT Theology to 'show us how to understand the OT as a unity' is similar to expecting the specialist in German literature 'to understand as a unity the product of more than a thousand years in the history of a people's thought and literature' (II.427). This supposed parallel must be questioned. For von Rad has

admitted that the OT has a focal point in Yahweh. It was also preserved and collected as religious literature. It was (with the possible
exception of the Wisdom Literature) written by a people who was
seeking to understand themselves as a unity (II.415, cf. I.118). It
can also be considered as Israel's witness to Yahweh's revelation of
himself. Finally, as H. H. Rowley pointed out, the different parts
were re-edited in one period as the sacred writings of a religious
community.[79] In these respects at least von Rad's comparison must
be queried. There are considerations which suggest that it is
reasonable to expect more of a unity than should be found in
German literature.[80]

The second objection is more factual. It is expressed in various
ways throughout the *Theology* but can be summarized as follows.
Eichrodt's type of Theology is unacceptable to von Rad because
'the traditio-historical aspect revealed a further aspect, the so-
called aspect of actuality' (II.413). In other words, the 'arbitrary
actualizations' of old traditions means it is impossible to look for
unity of ideas. As usual von Rad overstates the newness of the
discovery of these actualizations, for Eichrodt too was aware of
most of them. More significantly, he assumes they were arbitrary,
which is really the point at issue. Fohrer has argued that in the case
of the prophets the traditions were used to *express* their convictions
in such a way that they would have the maximum impact on their
hearers. This means that the ideas therein expressed would not be
arbitrary even though the actualizations of the traditions used
appeared to be.[81] R. J. Thompson says that for the Pentateuch
'the constant repetition and restatement of the tradition in worship and life must have proceeded on *some principle*.'[82] G. E. Wright
is evidence that even those who agree with von Rad in empha-
sizing 'Acts of God' need not reject the unity of the OT as well. He
says, 'There is something more fundamental in the Bible than
variety.'[83] It is of course Eichrodt's case that there may be some
rationale behind these 'arbitrary actualizations' and that we should
not *assume* there is no explanation.

A more cogent objection, which may underlie von Rad's criticisms, although it is not expressed, is that Israel's theologians were
not concerned with 'inner agreement'. So, in seeking to express
the unity of the OT we are engaged in a pursuit which did not
concern her. But, to claim, as Eichrodt does, that there are connections between apparently disparate ideas is not to claim that

Israelites were aware of them. Equally, even if Israelites were unaware of them, this does not mean there are no connections.
Indeed, if von Rad is correct to claim that Israel's theological
thinking is 'absolutely lacking in theological "systematics" ' (I.
116), then we can expect to discover links between 'arbitrary
actualizations' of which they were unaware but which are significant for our more conceptual approach. The construction of these
connections would represent the sub-structure of Israel's theology.
It would be immensely valuable for us in our understanding of
her theology, even if it would have been largely unconscious to
Israel.

In view of the above considerations, von Rad's objections do
not invalidate the attempt to look for the unity of the OT as
Eichrodt understands this, that is, how each part of the OT contributes towards a total picture.[84] We may feel (as von Rad hints)
that concern with the unity of the OT will lead us to an improper
exclusion of OT material which does not fit the 'total picture'.
This is a danger which is not always avoided by Eichrodt, but our
examination of the biblical material used in the two *Theologies*
showed that Eichrodt used a similar range of material to von
Rad.[85] The pre-eminent difficulty with Eichrodt's position is that
the total picture to which the individual elements contribute may
be selected subjectively, though this was not Eichrodt's intention.
Nevertheless, the search for and presentation of such unity as is
discovered is legitimate, even if no ultimate and final picture is ever
likely to be achieved.

5. *Old Testament Theology and the Concept of Revelation*

The last issue we are going to consider is that of the understanding
of revelation within the *Theologies*. There are several reasons for
this. The return to OT Theology was connected with the belief in
the 'theological' as distinct from the merely 'religious' value of the
OT. This means that the concept of revelation has played an
important part in contemporary OT Theologies.[86] Then, an
examination of this issue brings together the points we have
already considered and helps us to understand why the *Theologies*
were written as they were. Especially in Eichrodt's case, where
'revelation' appears to be an unexamined assumption, much of the
weakness of the *Theologies* becomes apparent.

Ideally we should distinguish several aspects of this issue. First, there is the understanding of the content, nature and mode of revelation which is held by our authors. Then, there is their understanding of the OT's view of revelation. Thirdly, there is the ways these are related in their *Theologies*, and finally we could consider the ways, if any, in which 'revelation' should be an integral part of a Theology. In both *Theologies* it is difficult to distinguish the first two aspects which makes any assessment of the third point problematic.

(a) Eichrodt

Eichrodt does not raise the question as to how far the OT was concerned with revelation. This is partly because he holds that OT religion is a religion of revelation. He tells us that the Exodus and Sinai covenant

> meant that man's relationship with God was based on revelation in the strict sense of the word – that is to say, on God's imparting of himself through the contingency of historical circumstance (I. 292).

Historical circumstances involve location in time and space which distinguishes revelation from 'the general ruck of possible religious ideas' (I. 371). Revelation thus contrasts with 'timeless truths' (I. 370)[87] and with 'any attempt to base a doctrine of God on general concepts or principles derived from human experience' (I. 292). Eichrodt not only believes that Israel thought she had special knowledge of God, but that she was right to think this. The consequence of the fact of revelation (*die Tatsache der Offenbarung*) is that 'Israel acquires in very truth a special position among the nations' (I. 369, cf. II. 415). The revelation, begun at Sinai,[88] continued throughout Israel's history and was always the consequence of an experience of God or his attributes. Eichrodt is very fond of the 'experience of God' and it occurs in many constructions, including 'their experience of the God of Sinai . . .' (I. 259, 346, 351, 406, etc.), 'their experience of Yahweh's control of history . . .' (I. 231, 453 II. 49, 71, etc.), 'the overpowering experience of God's positive control in the present . . .' (I. 192, cf. 283, 353, etc.), 'personal experience of God . . .' (I. 168, cf. 265, 343), 'general experience of God . . .' (I. 214) and the 'experience of a powerful moral will of God' (I. 77). This experience may have greater or lesser immediacy; the prophets represent one pole and the priests the other, but each type 'is rooted in a distinctive experience of God . . .' (I. 498, cf. I. 436, II. 162). Whilst 'the one God yet reveals himself in different ways in the different periods of human history' he does it 'without at the same time qualifying the reality of his fellowship' (I. 284). As revelation must be an experience of God by a human being, it becomes 'human experience' but Eichrodt does not tell us how such human experiences can be distinguished from those which contrast with revelation (I. 292).

There is also a lack of clarity about the relationship of human thought to revelation.[89] Revelation depends on an experience of God but it must be appropriated and applied to various realms. There is a struggle to reach the proper understanding of revelation (I.490). God's revelation only 'provides the material which, when willingly accepted, leads to a clarification and enrichment of human knowledge' (I. 222, cf. I. 75 n. 3, II. 324f.). This material is pre-eminently given in the Sinai revelation of the covenant God, and his impress can be seen on law and morality (I. 36, 259, 518, II. 71, 326, 369, 415, 474), the cultus (I.406), the understanding of the world (II. 15, 28, 49), of sin and punishment (II. 416, 425), of life and death (II.497), as well as the understanding of God as personal (I. 213, 286ff.), because the original revelation was applied to these realms. Further, according to his methodological section, human thought is needed to interpret events and to reason from law and cult (I.33). Again, the 'metaphysical attributes' are conceptualized on the basis of men's experiences of God (II. 185). Most surprising of all, 'the deepest insights Israel was ever to receive in her knowledge of revelation' were the results of using a *reductio ad absurdum* argument (II. 267). All of this suggests that the human mind was an important vehicle of revelation. On the other hand, reason seems to be the antithesis of revelation.[90] Philosophical speculation contrasts with 'the experience of God's close and living reality' (I. 227), 'a doctrine of God' based 'on general concepts or principles derived from human experience' with the reality of revelation (I.292). The historical nature of revelation distinguishes it from 'any moralistic re-interpretation or mystical sublimation' (I.371). The will of God is 'not worked out conceptually from any speculations or deductive processes whatever' (I.286), the divine reality 'is ultimately beyond reason and therefore only to be expressed in contradictory formulations' (I. 205), the Mosaic conception of God includes contradictions and is not 'the product of logical construction' (I. 111). It is difficult to reconcile these two attitudes to the place of the human mind in the process of revelation. Even the fundamental covenant revelation was, according to Eichrodt, the work of Moses' mind using a 'concept of long standing' (I. 37).

One of Eichrodt's motives for minimizing the part played by the human mind is to establish the facticity and givenness of revelation, which distinguishes Israel's beliefs from her neighbours' and which he hopes will help him to establish that the OT should be treated theologically. We have seen that he brings out the unique features of Israel's beliefs and traces these back to the covenant God. He does not discuss the possibility that ideas and institutions which Israel 'borrowed' and did not greatly modify might already be 'revelation', even though he says that 'Israel shared the conception of God common to the whole of the ancient East' (I.259), nor that ideas which she did alter might, on that account, be less accurate descriptions of God, nor does he discuss how far ideas which Israel borrowed were a contributory factor in the process of revelation. But if God could reveal himself in the 'contingency of historical events' why could he not use ideas and traditions about deities as a means of his revelation?[91] Occasionally Eichrodt allows that other religions had 'knowledge of God' (I. 413, II.425), but this is probably in a neutral sense, i.e. the understanding of deity. Fundamentally, revelation belongs to Israel alone.

Here again, this conflicts with one of his lines of argument. From time to time he uses comparative religion to defend Israel's faith. He brushes aside 'a depreciatory assessment' of the 'fear of God': 'A moment's consideration, however, of *the universal importance of fear in all religions* may be sufficient warning against such a step' (II.269, cf. e.g. I.178, 187, 275). Such an argument presupposes that to some extent all religions are valid, for to show that Israel held false beliefs about deity common to other religions is no commendation.

Eichrodt does not define what he means by revelation, nor does he investigate what the OT understood by it, nor how important it was for the OT. The relation between human experiences of God and ordinary experience is not clarified, nor is the relationship between revelation and human thought processes or comparative religion.

(b) Von Rad

Von Rad uses words like 'revelation' frequently,[92] but usually, and this is especially true for the OT section, in a neutral sense with no suggestion that revelation was Revelation.[93] It can be used of pagan religions: their use of images tells us 'how the deity is pleased to reveal himself, for the image is first and foremost the bearer of revelation' (I.214). His definition of myth is 'a timeless revelation taking place in the natural cycle' (I.139, cf. II.340). This would be an unacceptable use of 'revelation' for Eichrodt.[94] Further, when von Rad uses it of the biblical material, it is normally as an explication of the content, hence it occurs most frequently in descriptions of the Sinai revelation, the Torah in Deuteronomy, and the reception of revelation by the prophets.

In his section on the relation of the two Testaments he appears less reserved:

This self-revelation of God thus 'comes about in history', and it does so in the form of words and acts of God . . . It is in this way alone – and therefore an extremely non-speculative way – that knowledge of God was attained in Israel . . . God revealed himself by means of his words and . . . of his acts. Much has been written about the variety of forms which revelation by word could assume in Israel . . . It seems more difficult to answer the question of the way in which the knowledge of God given in his acts was attained. However, the OT believes that God always and for ever 'glorified himself' in his acts . . . (II.358).

Here, it is possible, although not necessary, that von Rad is hinting at his own commitment. First, he uses 'God' not 'Israel's God or 'Yahweh'. Secondly, the discrepancy between his claim that it is difficult to know how revelation was given in acts and that the OT believed God's activity was made visible 'beyond all possible doubt'[95] suggests that the difficulty is for our understanding of revelation.[96] Again, when a few pages later he writes, 'God's revelation in Israel was determined by a fellowship he initiated with an act of election' (II.372), he seems committed to the validity of the view. In spite of these possible exceptions, von Rad's general standpoint is different from Eichrodt's.

Von Rad is also less sure than Eichrodt about the mode of revelation: 'As things now are, it is quite impossible to express her understanding of revelation in a sentence' (II.416). In the case of the prophets' reception of revelation 'much that we should like to know is left unanswered' (II.59), although he offers the suggestion that sometimes 'revelation was a mental process' (II.67).

Von Rad does not define revelation, he indicates that our knowledge of the mode of revelation is restricted and he offers no indication of how the 'revelation' in the OT should be separated from the totality of Israel's beliefs.[97] Indeed, such a procedure would be out of line with von Rad's understanding. For him, revelation in the OT is not something given for all times. God's revelation, whether of his will for Israel, or of future acts, is always for a specific time. The way Israel made such past revelations relevant for a new situation was to re-actualize them in the light of the contemporary experience, and to view the present experiences in the light of the old traditions. Hence, the OT gains revelational value for us only when its traditions are reinterpreted in the light of the Christ-event. Whether we can be content to actualize in terms of Christ, whose history relates specifically to the first century AD, or whether in our turn we must re-actualize all the traditions in terms of our present, von Rad does not say. The logic of his *Theology* suggests the latter, but his treatment of the OT/NT implies the former.

Even if we were to accept all von Rad's arguments and to agree that this procedure were one way of giving theological significance to the OT, it would not establish that it was the only way. Just as the modern historical method has a different way of 'doing history' from Israel, neither of which can be dispensed with, so an account of OT theology, along Eichrodt's lines, could be considered an appropriate way for us to do OT theology.

Conclusion

What can be said about the part that a concern with revelation can legitimately play in an OT Theology? Does any commitment to this necessarily mean that OT Theology must forfeit its right to be considered 'scientific'? It seems to me that something like Eichrodt's approach does provide a legitimate presentation of the OT's theological content which is also relevant to the question of the revelational content of the OT. By giving a place to the unity and uniqueness of the OT and its relation to the NT, a frame of reference is provided which enables those who would see the final test of revelation within the NT to assess how far the OT approaches, anticipates and predicts the revelation of God through Jesus Christ. Of course, to remain 'scientific' all the claims made must be subject to the normal channels of research and refutation. No esoteric epistemology is necessary, and if some form of organized presentation is used, this need involve no ahistorical distortions, or necessitate any special concessions.

This does not mean that Eichrodt's *Theology* fulfils adequately all of these demands. Clearly it fails to some extent because Eichrodt was not sufficiently aware of his concept of revelation. Again, even a successful presentation would not amount to proof that the OT is revelational, all it need mean was that there are some noticeable similarities between the OT and the NT. But such a presentation would be relevant to the wider realm of Christian theology and would justify its description and separation from a history of Israel's religion. Thus, Eichrodt's basic conception of the purpose and function of an OT Theology seems more acceptable than von Rad's.

V

CONCLUSIONS

In making our comparative examination of the *Theologies* of Eichrodt and von Rad we have concentrated on their explicit arguments and have not considered, for instance, the contribution of their own Christian traditions to their *Theologies*. However, it would seem quite probable that Eichrodt's Calvinistic background played some part in his decision to make 'covenant' the dominating concept and there are certainly traces of Lutheranism in von Rad's *Theology*, although this is more noticeable in his commentary on *Genesis* and in *Wisdom in Israel*. Such considerations are quite legitimate, but we have avoided them, partly because it is less speculative to deal with the surface arguments, but more importantly, because our primary interest has been the nature of OT Theology and not Eichrodt and von Rad as people, or indeed, the relative importance of their contributions to OT scholarship. We chose to compare these two because their *Theologies* raised many of the important issues about OT Theology.

In fact, there is little doubt that von Rad has made the more important contribution to the realm of OT scholarship. Nearly every new monograph has copious references to him and it is clear that his research has given great impetus to others, and not only within the OT field. The primary value of his *Theology* is that it contains a summary of his own and other research within the form-critical school. As one of the most fertile minds which have utilized this method, von Rad's *Theology* illustrates its value. In his hands the OT text springs to life as we see the traditions reconnected with their real life situations and as we are made aware of the history of Israel's life which is often embedded in the traditions. Many reviewers have mentioned the freshness of von Rad's work and the 'living quality' of Israel's faith to which he directed us. His approach has delivered us from the apparent sterility of the literary analysts (although often it presupposes their work), by suggesting motives and methods which led to the composition of the OT as we now have it. He has also delivered us from over-preoccupation with 'personalities' of the OT (although perhaps he has gone too far in this direction) and with the 'original' text, for he has helped us to appreciate and understand the material we now have, as well as pointing out the limitations which this imposes on answering the sort of questions we might like answered. Undoubtedly, he had the great gift of pointing out the wood as well as the trees, by indicating the main thrust of a tradition. His *Theology* is a store house of exegetical insight and flashes of illumination. It is full of stimulating ideas and for the attentive reader there are many points where von Rad seems to be hinting at the relevance of Israel's theology for our predicament. Those who worked with him noticed his concern with details, but in many ways his *Theology* suggests that he had a poet's mind. These observations are not necessarily contradictory, for the poet strives to obtain a universal vision through the significance of the particular. His *Theology* then contributes a great deal to our understanding of the OT. Nevertheless it also betrays the defects of some of its qualities. Time and time again we have seen in it contradictions and ambiguities which suggest that he could not adequately synthesize the details in his mind or follow out the logic of his own position. Here is the real difference between him and Eichrodt. Whilst Eichrodt lacks the ingenuity, imagination and insight of von Rad, he has a comprehensiveness which few could match. Often his *Theology* is verbose, and sometimes it reads more like an apologetic sermon than a critical OT Theology, but no one can deny that it is a magnificent cathedral among OT studies. As a general work of reference to the many aspects of Israel's beliefs (and practice) as recorded within the OT it is hard to better. It has the advantage that it is not only comprehensive but also integrated, in that we are constantly reminded of the position of each tree in relationship to the whole wood. In comparison with earlier works, Eichrodt had shaken off the view that everything was accounted for if it was traced back to the most primitive level, and he tried to do justice to the various 'types' of religious life within Israel. His is a more open-minded approach than von Rad's: he is more open to other scholars'

opinions; he is more open to recognizing the influence and importance of those religions which surrounded Israel; he was more
open in his assessment of the proper content of an OT Theology.
To some extent, however, I regard his work as a theological
appreciation of Israel's religious history, rather than an OT
Theology, for very often it includes Eichrodt's reflections on her
history rather than an exposition. Eichrodt might well justify this
by claiming that the OT texts constantly direct us to that history.
Although his repeated emphasis on 'experience' gives it an old-
fashioned quality, it may well be that in these post-Barthian days,
when we are told that Schleiermacher is our contemporary, his
Theology will prove relevant. Yet, in many ways it is dated. Scholarship has moved on, archaeology has made immense strides and
comparative linguistics has become more important, whilst the
most his revisions have been able to do is to make mention of a tiny
fragment of this in his footnotes. It would take enormous courage
really to revise the whole work and any such revision would probably alter it beyond recognition.

In our investigation we had good cause to mention sociology.
I think it would be rewarding to compare Eichrodt's approach and
methods with those of sociology, especially with those of M.
Weber. In presenting a 'cross-section' Eichrodt did not simply
move from a religio-historical to a sociological approach, for it
would be a strange sociology which concentrated to the extent that
Eichrodt does on the religious beliefs of the society. Nevertheless,
there is a similarity, and a comparison would probably help us to
understand the truth claims of his *Theology*, i.e. at what levels and
in what ways the claims he makes are valid or invalid.

Although most of the time we have been contrasting the two
Theologies, it does seem to me that they are fundamentally similar,
not just because they use similar proportions of the different types
of OT material but because they are basically Deuteronomic. Both
'covenant' and *Heilsgeschichte* are strongly emphasized within the
Deuteronomic traditions and of course they are not unconnected.
Perhaps it is proper as well as probable that any adequate OT
Theology will be Deuteronomic, because of the influence of this
tradition on the OT, but neither scholar seems sufficiently aware
of this tendency, and increased awareness might help them to a
more positive appreciation of the post-exilic period.

Let us now return to our major interest, the nature of OT

Theology. We have seen that von Rad proposed a much more restricted task for an OT Theology, namely that of re-telling the traditions of the OT as they were understood by Israel, especially those of the *Heilsgeschichte*. The OT itself is ample evidence that Israel's theological concerns were not as restricted as this. Anyway, it proves impossible to separate *Heilsgeschichte* from the world of Israel's faith by anything other than an arbitrary decision, and *Heilsgeschichte* does not really fulfil von Rad's hopes because it cannot really be considered unique in any significant way. Of course, the NT links onto the OT's history, but it does not do this to the exclusion of other connections. In view of our analysis, I cannot consider that von Rad's *Theology* in any way supplants the Eichrodtian approach. It has summarized certain exegetical insights gained by form-criticism, although von Rad overstates both the validity of his views and the newness of them. Von Rad has suggested how Israel's theological deductions may have been made, but even if his general understanding is correct he has only indicated the surface connections and has not really probed the logic behind them or indeed the subconscious influences. Thus his is not even the only way of analysing Israel's theology.

On the whole, I consider that Eichrodt's conception of the function of an OT Theology is well able to withstand the shock-waves from von Rad's onslaught. His understanding of covenant certainly needs to be modified and I would not consider it the only organizing concept. As Eichrodt understands it – the God-Man relationship as revealed in the OT – it is both comprehensive enough and central enough to be useful. Equally, the concern with the unity and uniqueness of the OT and the relationship between the OT and the NT are legitimate interests which can be undertaken without necessarily prejudicing the objectivity of the work. A less ambiguous word for 'unity' might be either 'interrelation' or 'compatibility'. I also consider that both Eichrodt and von Rad overvalue that which is unique.

I am far less convinced about the way Eichrodt considers his *Theology* to warrant its title. Ultimately, I think he believes his work is a Theology because it expounds in an appropriate way (that is one which does not falsify or distort by incorporating non-biblical concepts) the record of the revelation of the one true God. He knows that besides being a record of revelation the OT is also the record of human views and failures, but he believes that by using the 'cross-section' method he will be able to eliminate this foreign matter from the revelation itself. We have already indicated that this method will only allow him to *present* what he considers to be essential. In many ways I would share his view that the OT contains a record of God's revelation to Israel, but I do not believe that my opinion could give Eichrodt's work its theological status. Rather its status is gained from its undergirding structure, which seeks to show to what extent the beliefs of the OT are continued or developed by the NT, especially (although I would add not only) where these views are unique and persistent. By its concerns with these issues an OT Theology is distinguished from a history of religion and, through the NT, is connected to the stream of Christian theology in general. It is not a scientific procedure just to accept the OT's claims to be revelational or just to believe this to be the case, as Eichrodt does. Rather, Eichrodt's general approach provides the material which *could be* cited as evidence for such a belief. Of course, this is not the only way of accounting for similarities between the two worlds of faith. Thus, I would not deny that Eichrodt's work deserves the name Theology, but I would stand the relationship between Eichrodt's beliefs and the structure of his *Theology* on its head. Along these lines it is possible for an OT Theology to be objective and to be of theological value.

NOTES

I INTRODUCTION

1. Cf. R. C. Dentan, *Preface to OT Theology* (revised edition), New York 1963; F. C. Prussner, *Methodology in OT Theology* (unpublished dissertation), Chicago 1952; H. J. Kraus, *Die biblische Theologie – Ihre Geschichte und Problematik*, Neukirchen 1970.

2. Those by Eichrodt, Köhler, Vriezen, Knight, Jacob, Procksch, van Imschoot and von Rad. An introduction to these can be found in R. B. Laurin (ed.), *Contemporary OT Theologians*, Valley Forge 1970 and W. Harrington, OP, *The Path of Biblical Theology*, Gill and Macmillan 1973.

3. Cf. the (incomplete) bibliography in R. C. Dentan's *Preface*.

4. There are more than a hundred reviews of these two Theologies, which indicates their importance. N. Porteous says, 'What is involved in all this discussion can best be appreciated by looking at the works of Eichrodt and von Rad', A. Richardson (ed.), *A Dictionary of Christian Theology*, London 1969, p. 209; cf. *Religious Studies* 3, 1967, p. 428; *ExpT* LXXIII, 1962, p. 142; G. E. Wright, *The OT and Theology*, New York 1969.

5. Cf. Select Bibliography, p. ix.

6. 'Hat die alttestamentliche Theologie noch selbständige Bedeutung innerhalb der alttestamentlichen Wissenschaft?', *ZAW* 47, 1929, pp. 83ff.

7. This view was based on recent German philosophy of history and appears to be similar to the so-called *perspectivism* of A. Richardson (cf. *History Sacred and Profane*, London 1964); it has been severely criticized by T. A. Roberts, *History and Christian Apologetics*, London 1960, pp. 46ff.; Van A. Harvey, *The Historian and the Believer*, London 1967; G. Downing, *The Church and Jesus* (SBT 2.10), 1968, pp. 141ff. (A more sympathetic evaluation is given by J. J. Navone SJ, *History and Faith in the Thought of Alan Richardson*, London 1966.) In fact, however, Eichrodt's position can be cleared of this criticism; indeed he demands that, 'prejudice, lack of discrimination and biased description' must be met 'with all the weapons that a scientific method provides', *ZAW* 47, 1929 p. 87.

8. For a fuller account of both Eissfeldt's and Eichrodt's essays, see N. W. Porteous, 'OT Theology', *The OT and Modern Study*, ed. H. H. Rowley, Oxford 1951, pp. 317ff.

9. Eichrodt holds that comparative religion is necessary for a full historical and theological appreciation of Israel's religion (I. 25).

10. Eichrodt probably depends on J. Wach (cf. *Religionswissenschaft,* Leipzig 1924, pp. 21, 192). Wach claims that this 'cross-section' would present the 'Being' (*Sein*) of a religion and the 'vertical section' (*Langschnitt*) the historical development. Yet the 'cross-section' is not directly normative, for that is the concern of the philosophy of religion. He says of these 'cross-sections' that the systematic study, interpretation and description should be dealt with by working from crucial central points, outwards. This recalls Eichrodt's reason for using the covenant (I. 17).

11. Cf. pp. 4f., 32f. below for suggestions on how a more favourable estimate of these covenants might affect Eichrodt's *Theology.*

12. Cf. esp. I. 13, *Religionsgeschichte Israels,* Bern 1969, p. 6, 'Prophet and Covenant', *Proclamation and Presence,* eds. J. I. Durham and J. R. Porter, London 1970, pp. 167ff.

13. Cf. N. W. Porteous, *OT and Modern Study,* p. 327.

14. For other suggestions by N. K. Gottwald, see *Contemporary OT Theologians,* pp. 45ff.

15. Cf. below p. 61.

16. For more details see *Gerhard von Rad: Seine Bedeutung für die Theologie,* München 1973. This consists of three lectures by H. W. Wolff, R. Rendtorff and W. Pannenberg.

17. For details of this method cf. e.g. K. Koch, *The Growth of the Biblical Tradition,* ET London 1969.

18. Cf. *The Problem of the Hexateuch and other Essays,* London 1966, pp. 1ff. For an evaluation of von Rad's position cf. E. W. Nicholson, *Exodus and Sinai in History and Tradition,* Oxford 1973, esp. pp. 1ff.

19. A tradition is a more or less fixed unit of material, often in narrative form, which may be used for many different purposes whilst the content remains basically unaltered.

20. In using both 'kerygma' and 'credo' von Rad was implying a parallel between the OT and the NT. The 'kerygma' is a number of significant 'events' in which and upon which the faith of a group of people is expressed and depends. The 'events' are linked together not on the basis of historico-critically established causal connections but because of their significance for the faith of the group.

21. 'Grundprobleme einer biblische Theologie des Alten Testaments', *TLZ* 68, 1943, col. 227.

22. Reprinted as 'Typological Interpretation of the OT', *Essays on OT Interpretation,* ed. C. Westermann, London 1963, pp. 17ff.

23. 'Das Grundprobleme der alttestamentlichen Theologie', *Theologie und Liturgie,* ed. L. Henning, Kassel 1952, pp. 29ff.

24. Cf. below p. 57.

25. His chapter on methodology (I. 105ff.) is structurally part of 'The Theology of Israel's Historical Traditions', but in view of references to the OT, it presumably applies to the whole *Theology.*

26. Cf. P. E. S. Thompson, 'The Yahwist Creation Story', *VTS* 21, 1971, pp. 197ff.

II EICHRODT'S THEOLOGY: COVENANT

1. For more detailed *surveys* of the field, cf. R. E. Clements, *Prophecy and Covenant* (SBT 43), 1965, *Abraham and David* (SBT 2. 5), 1967; D. R. Hillers, *Covenant: the History of a Biblical Idea*, Baltimore 1969. Fairly comprehensive bibliographies will be found in D. J. McCarthy, *Old Testament Covenant*, Oxford 1972, and his *Treaty and Covenant. A Study in Form in the Ancient Oriental Documents and in the* OT (Analecta Biblica 21), Rome 1963.

2. This is the title of the series in which McCarthy's book OT *Covenant* appeared.

3. First published 1921–24; ET, *The Psalms in Israel's Worship*, Oxford 1962.

4. First published 1938; ET in *The Problem of the Hexateuch*, pp. 1ff.

5. First published 1940; ET in *The Laws in Pentateuch and Other Studies*, Edinburgh 1966, pp. 1ff.

6. G. E. Mendenhall, 'Ancient Oriental and Biblical Law' *BA* 17, 1954, pp. 26ff., and 'Covenant Forms in Israelite Tradition', *BA* 17, 1954, pp. 50ff.

7. A. Phillips, *Ancient Israel's Criminal Law*, Oxford 1970; K. Baltzer, *The Covenant Formulary*, ET Oxford 1971.

8. R. E. Clements, *Prophecy*, p. 25.

9. Ibid., p. 119.

10. For history cf. J. Bright, *A History of Israel* (OTL), 1960, esp. p. 9; R. de Vaux, *Ancient Israel, Its Life and Institutions*, ET London 1965, p. 99.

11. It is often claimed that the wisdom literature is non-covenantal and there may be much truth in this. But von Rad's book, *Wisdom in Israel*, suggests that conceptually wisdom was not unrelated to the covenant as Eichrodt understood this. Further, the emphasis on the connection between Deuteronomy (the most covenant-orientated book in the OT) and scribal schools suggests that even the study of wisdom material will have to come to terms with covenant.

12. Cf. R. E. Clements, *Abraham*, p. 9.

13. D. J. McCarthy, 'Covenant in the OT: the Present State of Inquiry', *CBQ* 27, 1965, p. 220.

14. Cf. below pp. 69ff.

15. Cf. W. Zimmerli, *The Law and the Prophets*, ET Oxford 1965.

16. We have already pointed out that Eichrodt's concept studies are not as clear as they might be. There is considerable confusion in his discussion of covenant, along the lines indicated above, pp. 5f.

17. Eichrodt assumes that the word must originally have one meaning, for he develops both lines from the same starting point. Often words stand for more than one concept. In fact there was always a variety of covenant types: his two lines of development roughly correspond to the vassal type and the promissory type of covenants.

18. D. J. McCarthy, OT *Covenant*, p. 6.

19. Eichrodt claims that all secular covenants were bilateral (I. 37). The discovery of the promissory type might appear to invalidate this claim, but probably even the promissory covenants *implied* (but unlike the vassal treaties did not *state*) a certain attitude on the parties involved. Talk about

bilateral or unilateral covenants is confusing anyway. These terms might refer to the initiative for making the covenant (Gen. 31.44), the act which initiated it (Gen. 15.17ff.; 21.27), the relationship established by the act. Even if the status of the participants was unequal, the obligations could be mutual, i.e. to keep the peace (cf. Josh. 9), although such an obligation might benefit either the one or the other according to circumstances.

20. It is often supposed that once the validity of the parallel between Hittite Treaties and the Sinaitic covenant is accepted, that this will assist Eichrodt. He seems to believe this (cf. 'Covenant and Law', *Interpretation* 20, 1966, pp. 302ff.). In certain respects this is true, e.g. the connection of Exodus and Sinai, the place of law within and not as the presupposition for the covenant. But certain features, such as the claim for uniqueness, that it was covenant which gave rise to a sense of nationhood, and that God, as the initiator, was free to dissolve the relation, become less feasible.

21. For instance, it could be claimed that as this was how later Israelite theologians came to express their faith and traditions, it should be primary in an OT Theology, and would be useful for relating the development of traditions. The question about the historical relationship with Hittite treaties would also be less important. Clements perhaps implies, when he writes of an 'instructive parallel' (*Prophecy*, p. 70 n. 1, cf. *Abraham*, p. 9, 'usefully illuminated by . . . political treaties') that there does not have to be historical dependence for the treaties to help our understanding. Cf. McCarthy, *OT Covenant*, p. 85: 'The similarities are conceptual, not formal.' Further, this would mean that to expound the OT in terms of covenant one would not need to establish that features could *only* be explained on this basis, but merely that they *could be* so explained: contrast McCarthy's position.

22. The problem of the proper translation is a complex one, involving not only the analysis of the Hebrew but also of our languages. Köhler indicates that we may wish to change our translation of *bᵉrit* from 'covenant' to 'agreement' because the former has a theological flavour ('Problems in the study of the Language of the OT', *JSS* 1, 1956, p. 4). Lohfink and Clements have a similar understanding of Gen. 15, but whereas Lohfink refuses to refer to it as a covenant and insists that it is an oath (*Die Landverheissung als Eid*, Stuttgart 1967, ch. 10) Clements quite happily calls it a covenant (cf. *Abraham*, esp. pp. 15ff.). McCarthy calls the Hittite agreements 'treaties' and retains 'covenant' for the OT (*Treaty and Covenant*, p. 9). I suspect this is partly because he doubts whether they were historically linked. It is also worth bearing in mind that *Bund* is more frequently used in German than is 'covenant' in English, hence 'covenant' is freer than *Bund* to take its colouring from the biblical usage.

23. A. Jepsen, 'Berith. Ein Beitrag zur Theologie der Exilszeit', *Verbannung und Heimkehr*, ed. A. Kuschke, Tübingen 1961, pp. 161ff.

24. G. Fohrer, 'Der Mittelpunkt einer Theologie des Alten Testaments', *TZ* 24, 1968, pp. 161ff.

25. E. Kutsch, 'Probleme des alttestamentlichen Bundes begriffes', *ZAW* 79, 1967, pp. 18ff. Cf. *Verheissung und Gesetz* (BZAW 131), 1972.

26. D. J. McCarthy, *OT Covenant*, p. 81.

27. In 'Covenant and Law', Eichrodt deals with, or more accurately,

attempts to circumvent, the linguistic criticisms by appealing to the Hittite treaties. He does not really deal with the linguistic issues, especially those occasions when *berit* is parallel to 'oath'.

28. Cf. J. Bright, *History of Israel*, p.133; A. Alt, 'The Formation of the Israelite State in Palestine', *Essays on OT History and Religion*, ET Oxford 1966, p.195; R. E. Clements, *Abraham*, pp.52f.

29. *Treaty and Covenant*, pp.96ff.; cf. A. Nötscher, 'Bundesformular und "Amtschimmel"', *BZ* 9, 1965, p.192: 'A specific word for treaty appears to be lacking.'

30. 'Covenant', *IDB* I, p.716.

31. *The Covenant Formulary*, p.90 n.4. This is in fact disputed, cf. G. Quell, *TDNT* II, p.119; D. J. McCarthy, *Treaty and Covenant*, p.17; H. Lambert, 'Les "Reformis" d'Urukagina', *Revue d'Assyriologie et d'Archaeologie Orientale* 50, 1956, p.183.

32. Cf. D. J. McCarthy, *OT Covenant*, pp.32f.

33. Cf. W. Eichrodt, *Proclamation and Presence*, pp.173ff.

34. I.49: 'a remarkable *retrojection* of the covenant concept', cf. below, pp.25ff.

35. For summaries of the position, cf. J. Bright, *Early Israel in Recent History Writing* (SBT 19), 1956; H. Schmid, *Mose Überlieferung und Geschichte* (BZAW 110), 1968; R. Smend, *Das Mosebild von Heinrich Ewald bis Martin Noth*, Tübingen 1959; E. Oswald, *Das Bild Mose in der kritischen alttestamentlichen Wissenschaft seit J. Wellhausen*, Berlin 1962.

36. Cf. K. Koch, 'The concept *Stiftungsreligion* indicates nothing other than the revelational character of Moses' message . . .', 'Tod des Religionstifters', *KuD* 8, 1962, pp.104f.; cf. F. Baumgärtel, 'Der Tod des Religionstifters' *Kud* 9, 1963, pp.223ff.; R. Rendtorff, 'Die Entstehung der israelitischen Religion als religionsgeschichtliches und theologisches Problem', *TLZ* 88, 1963, cols. 735ff.

37. Cf. *Religionsgeschichte Israels*, pp.13ff.

38. Cf. e.g. I.72, 'even in circles where the idea of a written transmission . . . is regarded with scepticism . . .'

39. For Eichrodt, cf. J. Bright, *History of Israel*.

40. G. Kline solves the enigma that the Hittite treaty form is clearest in Deuteronomy by arguing for a Mosaic date; cf. *The Treaty of the Great King. The Covenant Structure of Deuteronomy*, Grand Rapids 1963.

41. In Deuteronomy the covenant is made at Horeb, not Sinai, e.g. Deut. 5.2.

42. D. J. McCarthy, *CBQ* 27, 1965, p.229; cf. *Treaty and Covenant*, pp.129ff.

43. M. Smith, 'The Present State of OT Studies', *JBL* 88, 1969, p.30.

44. *Treaty and Covenant*, p.122.

45. Ibid., p.121; cf. R. Frankena, 'The Vassal Treaties of Esarhaddon and the Dating of Deuteronomy', *Oudtestamentische Studiën* 14, 1965, pp.122ff.; M. Weinfeld, 'Traces of Assyrian Treaty Formulae in Deuteronomy', *Biblica* 46, 1965, pp.417ff.

46. Cf. now D. R. Hillers, *Covenant: the History of a Biblical Idea*, Baltimore 1969, pp.157f.

47. It is possible to develop this line of argument further by seeing in Deuteronomy the development of the Sinaitic traditions, all of which are dependent on the Hittite treaties. Cf. below pp. 21ff.

48. Cf. e.g. H. J. Kraus, *Worship in Israel*, ET Oxford 1966, pp. 136ff.

49. First emphasized by M. Noth, *Das System der zwölf Stämme Israels*, Stuttgart 1930; for its importance cf. his 'The Laws in the Pentateuch'.

50. Cf. D. G. Spriggs, *Towards an Understanding of OT Theology* (unpublished dissertation), Oxford 1971, pp. 355f.

51. Cf. D. J. McCarthy, *OT Covenant*, pp. 8, 63ff.

52. Ibid, p. 65 n. 21.

53. Cf. L. Perlitt, *Bundestheologie im Alten Testament*, Neukirchen 1969; C. F. Whitley, 'Covenant and Commandment in Israel', *JNES* 22, 1963, pp. 42ff.

54. Eichrodt appears rather sceptical about this second point, cf. *Proclamation and Presence*, p. 175.

55. R. E. Clements, *Prophecy*, p. 8; cf. also J. L. Mays, *Amos* (OTL), 1969, *Hosea* (OTL), 1969.

56. Cf. e.g. H. B. Huffmon, 'The Covenant Lawsuit in the Prophets', *JBL* 78, 1959, pp. 285ff.; C. Fensham, 'Malediction and Benediction in Ancient Near Eastern Vassal Treaties and the OT' *ZAW* 74, 1962, pp. 1ff.; D. R. Hillers, *Treaty Curses and the OT Prophets*, Rome 1964.

57. Cf. *OT Covenant*, p. 40.

58. In *Proclamation and Presence*, pp. 184ff., he suggests that it is not the covenant concept but the prophetic experience of God which is all important, but, of course, this experience was the experience of the covenant God.

59. *OT Covenant*, p. 79.

60. C. F. Whitley (whose *The Prophetic Achievement*, London 1963, pp. 26ff., provides the most accessible account of the position of those who maintain the prophets were not dependent on any covenant concept, because this was a Deuteronomic innovation) insists that the Exodus and Sinai traditions were distinct. Even if this were originally the case, they were surely firmly integrated well before the time of the writing prophets, as both J and E show. (Cf. *Towards an Understanding of OT Theology*, pp. 134ff. for an analysis and critique of Whitley's position.)

61. Cf. e.g. H. Reventlow, *Wächter über Israel: Ezekiel und seine Tradition* (BZAW 82), 1962.

62. Cf. e.g. S. Mowinckel, op. cit.; A. Weiser, The Psalms (OTL), 1962; H. J. Kraus, op. cit.; W. Beyerlin, *Origins and History of the Oldest Sinaitic Tradition*, ET Oxford 1965.

63. G. E. Mendenhall, *BA* 17, 1954, pp. 26ff., 50ff.

64. Cf. G. von Rad, *Problem of the Hexateuch*, pp. 1ff. For Eichrodt's violent reaction see I. 512ff.

65. D. J. McCarthy, *Treaty and Covenant*, pp. 30ff., *OT Covenant*, p. 26 n. 29; H. B. Huffmon, *CBQ* 27, 1965, p. 109 n. 41; A. F. Campbell, 'An Historical Prologue in a Seventh Century Treaty', *Biblica* 50, 1969, pp. 535f.; K. Deller and S. Parpola, 'Ein Vertrag Assurbanipalis mit dem arabischen Stamm Qudar', *Orientalia* 37, 1968, pp. 464ff.

66. Cf. however, *OT Covenant*, p. 16: 'If anything, there is perhaps evi-

dence for some sort of ritual in Israel which followed a sequence rather like that of the ancient Hittite treaty.'

67. Cf. G. E. Mendenhall, op. cit., p. 59.

68. E. Gerstenberger, 'Covenant and Commandment', *JBL* 84, 1965, pp. 38ff. For a summary of current opinion on the Decalogue, cf. J. J. Stamm and M. E. Andrew, *The Ten Commandments in Recent Research*, (SBT 2. 2), 1967.

69. Cf. E. Nielsen, *The Ten Commandments in New Perspective* (SBT 2. 7), 1968, p. 73; A. Phillips, *Ancient Israel's Criminal Law*, is devoted to expounding the Decalogue as a covenant document of a special kind.

70. Cf. P. B. Harner, 'Exodus, Sinai and Hittite Prologues', *JBL* 85, 1966, pp. 233ff.

71. *OT Covenant*, pp. 30f., cf. *Treaty and Covenant*, pp. 153ff.

72. W. Zimmerli, 'Erwägungen zum "Bund"', *Wort – Gebot – Glaube*, *Eichrodt Festschrift*, ed. H. J. Stoebe, AThANT 59, 1970, pp. 171ff.; J. Begrich, 'Berit. Ein Beitrag zur Erfassung einer alttestamentlichen Denkform', *ZAW* 60, 1944, pp. 1ff.

73. This contrasts with his procedure over material from Deut. or P.

74. M. Newman, *The People of the Covenant*, London 1965; J. R. Porter, *Moses and Monarchy, A Study in the Biblical Tradition of Moses*, Oxford 1963.

75. Op. cit., p. 51. Newman is prepared to reconstruct an original event which corresponds closely to Eichrodt's analysis. However, he would emphasize the theophanic nature of the initiation of the covenant (op. cit. pp. 29ff. esp. p. 30 n. 19, and 32 n. 24; cf. *OT Covenant*, pp. 31, 73).

76. This, not merely in the sense that much of it could exist independently of the covenant theme (e.g. concept studies, summary of law, descriptions of OT offices and sacrifices) but as a theology of covenant.

77. Cf. above p. 15.

78. In many ways it is possible to consider Eichrodt's *Theology* Deuteronomistic, not only because of the place given to the Mosaic covenant, but also, for instance, because it is a combination of prophetic and priestly approaches, with an eschatological orientation, because of its concern for unity and its subordination of wisdom traditions and the monarchy to the covenant tradition. Many other points can also be supplied. Is this the ultimate reason why Eichrodt cannot accept the post-exilic period?

79. Cf. Isa. 29.22; Micah 7.20; Pss. 47.9; 105.42–44. The pre-exilic date of all these passages is disputed.

80. Cf. R. E. Clements, *Abraham*, for justification and expansion of this paragraph. Relevant bibliographical details will also be found there. Cf. also D. J. McCarthy, *OT Covenant* pp. 45ff., 80ff.

81. Cf. R. E. Clements, op. cit.

82. Ibid., pp. 15ff., 47ff.

83. Ibid., pp. 50ff. I am by no means as sure as Clements that the Abrahamic traditions were restricted to Hebron. I would, however, accept that Hebron was probably the major, but not the sole, channel through which the Abrahamic traditions were connected with David.

84. Ibid. pp. 53f., 71.

85. Cf. now K. Seybold, *Das davidische Königtum im Zeugnis der Propheten* (FRLANT 107), 1972, e.g. pp. 163ff.

86. Cf. Ex. 34.10.

87. Cf. Gen. 15.7; II Sam. 7.8–9.

88. Cf. Isa. 55.3–5. On this passage cf. O. Eissfeldt, 'The Promise of Grace to David in Isa. 55.1–5', *Israel's Prophetic Heritage, Muilenburg Festschrift*, eds. B. W. Anderson and W. Harrelson, London 1962, pp. 196ff. Note too, that in some psalms (e.g. Ps. 72) and the Deuteronomic History, the prosperity of Israel depends upon the obedience of the king to Yahweh.

89. Cf. J. R. Porter, op. cit., pp. 16f.

90. Even Ps. 132 holds that the covenant is 'for ever', cf. v. 12.

91. Cf. R. E. Clements, *Abraham*, pp. 76f.

92. Ibid., p. 34.

93. A similar picture emerges from Gen. 15.1–6, if the cultic background of *ḥšb* is recalled; cf. G. von Rad, 'Faith Reckoned as Righteousness', *Problem of the Hexateuch*, pp. 125ff.

94. Cf. R. E. Clements, op. cit., p. 73. He, and others, seem to minimize the conditional nature of the Abrahamic covenant.

95. Other passages, such as Ps. 105 (which could well be pre-exilic – contrast R. E. Clements, op. cit., p. 64 – because of its unclouded optimism about the possession of the land), Ezek. 33.23ff., and Gen. 26.1–6, also suggest that this covenant was understood to be conditional.

96. H. Gese, 'Der Davidsbund und die Zionserwählung', *ZTK* 61, 1964, pp. 10ff., suggests that this covenant is the reward for bringing the ark of Yahweh to Jerusalem.

97. Cf. A. Johnson, *Sacral Kingship in Ancient Israel*, Cardiff 1967; G. Widengren, 'King and Covenant', *JSS* 2, 1957, pp. 1ff.; A. Phillips, op. cit., esp. pp. 164f. Contrast G. von Rad, 'The Royal Ritual in Judah', *Problem of Hexateuch*, pp. 222ff.

98. Cf. G. von Rad, *Problem of the Hexateuch*, p. 62; R. E. Clements, *Prophecy*, p. 64; contrast R. E. Clements, *Abraham*, p. 33.

99. Cf. W. Zimmerli, 'Sinaibund und Abrahambund' *TZ* 16, 1960, pp. 268ff.; P. R. Ackroyd, *Exile and Restoration* (OTL), 1968, pp. 95f.

100. R. de Vaux, 'Le Roi d'Israël, vassal de Yahvé', *Tisserant Festschrift*, Studie e Testi 231, Rome 1964, pp. 119ff.

101. D. J. McCarthy, *OT Covenant*, pp. 50f., 84f.; contrast K. Seybold, op. cit., pp. 40ff.

102. Cf. O. Eissfeldt, *The OT. An Introduction*, ET Oxford 1966, p. 539; M. Noth, *Überlieferungsgeschichtlichen Studien* I, Tübingen, 1957, p. 175; contrast A. M. Brunet, 'La Theologie du Chroniste, théocratie et messianisme' *Sacra Pagina* I, Paris 1959, pp. 384ff.; R. J. North, 'The Theology of the Chronicler', *JBL* 82, 1963, pp. 369ff.

103. Contrast von Rad, I.157; D. J. McCarthy, *OT Covenant*, p. 47.

104. Op cit., p. 381 n. 1.

105. H. J. Kraus, *Worship*, pp. 183ff., M. Noth, *Laws*, pp. 132ff., M. Newman (op. cit., p. 152) suggests that the J Sinai covenant legend was used at Hebron, so that mutual influence could already have been operative.

106. Cf. F. C. Fensham, 'Covenant, Promise and Expectation' *TZ* 23, 1967, p. 314; A. Phillips, op. cit., p. 163.

III VON RAD'S THEOLOGY: HEILSGESCHICHTE

1. In the ET there are 139 references to saving history. Sometimes this is a translation of *heilsgeschichtlich*, although usually of *Heilsgeschichte*. Once *Heilsgeschichte* is translated 'sacred history' (ET II. 226). Further, on ET I. 170 there is no translation equivalent at all for *heilsgeschichtlich* (cf. German I[5]. 184).

2. Cf. above pp. 17f., 10.

3. Cf. J. P. Martin, *The Last Judgment*, Edinburgh 1963, pp. 170ff.

4. Cf. German II[5]. 441 and O. Cullmann, *Salvation in History*, ET London 1967, p. 77.

5. O. Cullmann (op. cit.) attempts to define his term. He has sympathy for von Rad's position (pp. 53f.), so it is tempting to use his account to understand von Rad. However, whilst Cullmann is prepared to compare 'salvation history' and 'objective history', von Rad, especially in the early stages, insisted on their total separation.

6. 'Antwort auf Conzelmanns Fragen', *EvTh* 24, 1964, p. 399.

7. C. A. Keller, *TZ* 17, 1961, p. 368, reviewing von Rad's *Theology*, K. Koch, *The Growth of the Biblical Tradition*, ET London 1969, p. 62; C. Barth, *EvTh* 23, 1963, pp. 356f.; J. A. Soggin, *TLZ* 89, 1964, col. 725; F. Baumgärtel, *TLZ* 86, 1961, col. 811, also reviewing von Rad's *Theology*.

8. 'Formulated the phenomenon' (*das Phänomen der Heilsgeschichte klar formuliert*), is a curious expression. Normally one formulates ideas, concepts, etc. and describes phenomena. Does this conflation indicate that von Rad is avoiding the question as to whether *Heilsgeschichte* is a conceptual or an objective reality? Cf. his avoidance of the question of historicity in relation to saving history (see below pp. 49ff.).

9. Cf. von Rad, *TLZ* 68, 1943, col. 227.

10. M. Honecker, 'Zum Verständnis der Geschichte in G. von Rads Theologie des Alten Testaments', *EvTh* 23, 1963, p. 148.

11. Cf. I. 350, 281, etc.

12. Cf. above p. 36.

13. In German II[5]. 329, this has been changed. Nevertheless, it is proper to consider this in an attempt to understand what he meant.

14. Cf. II. vi and above p. 34.

15. G. von Rad, *Wisdom in Israel*, p. 257.

16. Perhaps von Rad might mean that it lacks the concern to understand the present in the light of the past by re-actualizing the traditions. But, in his way, Ben Sirach is surely suggesting, by his list of famous men from the past, what the men of his day should strive after, cf. Ecclus. 44.10ff.

17. Th. C. Vriezen, in what is the best single discussion of von Rad's *Theology*, points out that there is a similar ambivalence over the relation between history and *Heilsgeschichte*. There, as here, this is partly the result of modifications von Rad has made in response to criticisms, but partly it is inherent in his initial position. Cf. 'Geloof, openbaring en geschiedenis in de nieuwste Oud-Testamentische Theologie', *Kerk en Theologie* 16, 1965, pp. 97–113, 210–218.

18. Many scholars accept that von Rad has emphasized an important element of Israel's faith, or the way she expressed it, but cannot accept von Rad's exclusive position. Cf. e.g. R. C. Dentan, *JBL* 82, 1963, p. 106: 'While it is true that a concern with God's action in history is uniquely characteristic of OT religion, it by no means follows that the "theology" of the OT can, or should be, discussed only in these terms.'

19. J. Barr, *JSS* 4, 1959, pp. 286ff., *ExpT* LXXIII, 1962, pp. 142ff., and esp. 'Revelation in the OT and in modern Theology', *New Theology* 1, eds. M. E. Matty and D. G. Peerman, New York 1964, pp. 60ff., and *Old and New in Interpretation*, London 1966, pp. 65–102.

20. *Old and New,* p. 72.

21. Ibid., p. 73.

22. On occasions he stigmatizes material which lacks this connection, e.g. I. 363: 'The Enthronement Psalms are the least "Israelite" poems.'

23. I believe that this is also true for prophecy, cf. below pp. 56ff.

24. *Old and New*, pp. 74ff.

25. C. Barth, 'Grundprobleme einer Theologie des Alten Testaments', *EvTh* 23, 1963, pp. 368f.

26. Cf. F. Baumgärtel, *TLZ* 86, 1961, col. 896 n. 4.

27. In German II[5] there are considerable changes to the discussion of Apocalyptic. Our examination is based on the ET for the convenience of readers familiar with this. In the alterations von Rad has tried to strengthen his case for the dependence of apocalyptic solely on wisdom, but it is still unconvincing. Cf. K. Koch, *The Rediscovery of Apocalyptic*, ET (SBT 2.22), 1972, pp. 42ff.; F. M. Cross, 'New Directions in the Study of Apocalyptic', *Journal for Theology and the Church* 6, 1969, pp. 157ff., esp. p. 159 n. 3; R. North, 'Prophecy to Apocalyptic via Zechariah', *VTS* 22, 1972, pp. 47ff.

28. Cf. P. D. Hanson, 'Jewish Apocalyptic Against its Near Eastern Environment', *Revue Biblique* 78, 1971, pp. 31ff.

29. N. Porteous, *Daniel* (OTL), 1965, p. 21; O. Eissfeldt, *The OT. An Introduction,* p. 528.

30. D. S. Russell, *The Method and Message of Jewish Apocalyptic* (OTL), 1964, p. 232.

31. H. H. Rowley, *The Relevance of Apocalyptic,* London 1950, p. 152. Cf. G. von Rad, *Wisdom in Israel*, pp. 263ff.

32. Cf. K. Koch, op. cit., p. 44.

33. Cf. H. H. Rowley, op. cit. pp. 37ff. Although von Rad lists Rowley's book he shows no sign of having read it! Cf. K. Koch, op. cit., p. 42.

34. K. Koch, op. cit., p. 140 n. 48.

35. Ibid., p. 46. For a fuller examination of this cf. P. von der Östen-Sacken, *Die Apokalyptik in ihren Verhältnis zu Prophetie und Weisheit* (Theologische Existenz heute 157), München 1969.

36. Cf. O. Plöger, *Theocracy and Eschatology*, ET Oxford 1968; W. Zimmerli, *Man and his Hope in the OT*, ET (SBT 2.20), 1972, pp. 140ff.

37. K. Koch, op. cit. p. 140 n. 144. Of course, such influences as these need not be derived *directly* from the so-called 'wisdom schools'.

38. J. Barr, *Old and New*, p. 77.

39. G. E. Wright, *The OT and Theology*, New York 1969, pp. 47ff.

40. Ps.99.6–8 does not fit into this scheme very well. Whilst there is contact with the 'event' by 'the pillar of cloud', it is the words which seem important.

41. Cf. J. Barr, *New Theology* 1, p.65.

42. J. Barr, *Old and New*, p.74 n.1; C. Carmichael, 'A New View of the Origin of the Deuteronomic Credo', *VT* 19, 1969, pp.273ff.; Th. C. Vriezen, op. cit., pp.214f.

43. Cf. e.g. I. Engnell, 'Methodological Aspects of OT Study', *VTS* 7, 1959, pp.13ff., esp. p.19.

44. B. Albrektson, *History and the Gods*, Lund 1967. Von Rad attempted to defend himself against Albrektson in *Wisdom in Israel*, p.290. He claimed Albrektson did not deal with 'the specific theological relevance of history'. I find this hard to accept in view of his chapters on 'The Divine Plan in History' and 'Historical Events as Divine Revelation'. Certainly, Albrektson does not concentrate on von Rad's favourites, the Yahwist and the Deuteronomic History.

45. Cf. B. Albrektson, op. cit., p.16.

46. Ibid., pp.116f.; J. R. Wilch, *Time and Event. An exegetical study of the use of* ʿeth *in the OT in comparison to other temporal expressions in clarification of the concept of time*, Leiden 1969.

47. Cf. B. Albrektson, op. cit., p.16.

48. Ibid., pp.24ff., 109ff.

49. Ibid. p.114.

50. Ibid., pp.94, 96.

51. Ibid., pp.115f.

52. Cf. below pp.49ff. Von Rad's comments in *Wisdom in Israel*, p.290, which emphasize the contingency of Israel's view of history in contrast to the 'schematic' view of the ancient Near East, indicates that he might believe this.

53. Rendtorff, 'Geschichte und Überlieferung', *Studien zur Theologie der alttestamentlichen Überlieferung*, eds. K. Koch and R. Rendtorff, Neukirchen 1961, p.91.

54. B. S. Childs, *Myth and Reality in the Old Testament* (SBT 27), 1960, p.75.

55. This confusion is not assisted by printing 'unlinear' for 'unilinear' (II.100), nor by the ET, although the translator had an extremely difficult task in this section.

56. Cf. J. Barr, *Biblical Words for Time* (SBT 33), 1962, pp.140f.

57. Cf. M. I. Finley, 'Myth, Memory and History', *History and Theory* 4, 1965, p.293: 'Time past consists of a number of individual events . . . time future consists of anticipated events or satisfaction . . .'; the scientific concept of time 'is largely meaningless for ordinary human purposes'.

58. Cf. J. Barr, op. cit., pp. 142f.

59. Wilch, op. cit., pp.170f.

60. Notice that when von Rad says that 'while the earth remains' is equivalent to 'for all time' and implies no limit, he is admitting that the idea of endless time was conceivable; this is surely one aspect of our abstract view of time.

61. This can be represented diagramatically as follows, where events are indicated by x and time by enclosed areas:

(1) events in random relationship to each other	(2) events in linear relationship to connected events, but sequences of events unrelated	(3) all events related to every other event as well as in significant sequence with certain events

62. G. F. Oehler, *Theology of the OT*, ET Grand Rapids 1883, pp. 9f.

63. Oehler, op. cit., p. 10.

64. Cf. A. Richardson, *History Sacred and Profane*, p. 233; E. Rust, *Review and Expositor* 64, 1967, p. 379. Contrast C. Barth, *EvTh* 23, 1963, p. 365. For von Rad, history is important, so although he appears to hold a position *vis-à-vis* the OT similar to that of Bultmann *vis-à-vis* the NT, he cannot justly be called an existentialist.

65. German II⁵, 1968, p. 444.

66. F. Hesse, 'Die Erforschung der Geschichte Israels als theologische Aufgabe', *KuD* 4, 1958, pp. 1ff., 'Kerygma oder geschichtliche Wirklichkeit', *ZTK* 59, 1960, pp. 17ff., 'Bewährt sich eine "Theologie der Heilstatsachen" am Alten Testament?', *ZAW* 81, 1969, pp. 1ff.; V. Maag, 'Historie und ausserhistorische Begrundung alttestamentlicher Theologie', *Schweizer Theologische Umschau* 29, 1959, pp. 6ff.; J. Hempel, *Bibliotheca Orientalia* 15, 1958, pp. 212ff. Cf. von Rad, German II¹, 1960, pp. 7ff.; H. Conzelmann, 'Fragen an G. von Rad', *EvTh* 24, 1964, pp. 113ff.; G. von Rad, 'Antwort auf Conzelmanns Fragen', *EvTh* 24, 1964, pp. 388ff.

67. J. A. Soggin, 'Geschichte, Historie und Heilsgeschichte im Alten Testament', *TLZ* 89, 1964, cols. 721ff., cf. 'Alttestamentliche Glaubenszeugnisse und geschichtliches Wirklichkeit', *TZ* 17, 1961, pp. 385ff.

68. J. Barr, *Old and New*, pp. 69f.

69. Th. C. Vriezen, *Kerk en Theologie* 16, 1965, p. 104. As Vriezen suggests, this raises the problem of which Israelite picture is normative.

70. Ibid., p. 106.

71. E. Rust, *Salvation History: a Biblical Interpretation*, Philadelphia 1963, p. 50; G. E. Wright, *God Who Acts* (SBT 8), 1952, p. 84; J. Bright, *Early Israel*, pp. 11f.; J. A. Soggin, *TLZ* 89, 1964, col. 734.

72. II¹. 8ff.

73. G. E. Wright, op. cit., pp. 126f.

74. C. Barth, op. cit., p. 368.

75. Cf. esp. R. Rendtorff, *Studien*, pp. 81ff.; 'Hermeneutik des Alten Testaments als Frage nach der Geschichte', *ZTK* 59, 1960, pp. 27ff.

76. Von Rad also thinks that Israel's faith is exempt from historical analysis, cf. I. 108, 'the phenomenon of the faith itself, which speaks now of salvation, now of judgment' is, for historical criticism, 'beyond its power to explain'. This is dubious anyway, but, as Baumgärtel points out, with the traditions we are not directly concerned with the faith itself, but with the expressions of that faith, cf. *TLZ* 86, 1961, col. 805.

77. Cf. articles already listed above.

78. *ZTK* 57, 1960, p. 9.

79. II¹ (German) p. 9; cf. M. Honecker, *EvTh* 23, 1963 p. 160.

80. *KuD* 4, 1958, pp. 13f.

81. The German is *Mass*. A more adequate translation would surely be, 'standard', the idea being that it must be evaluated on its own terms.

82. Cf. Eichrodt I. 50.

83. *OTI*, p. 26.

84. Cf. pp. 8f. above for some of the structural problems involved by this twofold division.

85. C. A. Keller, *TZ* 17, 1961, p. 367; cf. F. Baumgärtel, *TLZ* 86, 1961, cols. 808ff.

86. Cf. C. Barth, op. cit., pp. 369ff.

87. *VT* 13, 1963, p. 110; cf. von Rad I. 232ff.

88. Cf. I. 233; *Studies in Deuteronomy*, p. 69.

89. Cf. II. 3ff.

90. G. Fohrer, 'Remarks on the Modern Interpretation of the Prophets', *JBL* 80, 1961, pp. 309ff.; 'Tradition and Interpretation im AT', *ZAW* 73, 1961, pp. 1ff.

91. See the biblical indices.

92. Cf. F. Baumgärtel, *TLZ* 86, cols. 810f.

93. Cf. also *Studies in Deuteronomy*, pp. 82f.

94. It is entirely appropriate that this part should have been published separately.

95. It is noticeable that those who praise von Rad's treatment of the relationship between the testaments (e.g. K. Schwarzwäller, 'Das Verhältnis Altes Testament-Neues Testament im Lichte der gegenwärtigen Bestimmungen', *EvTh* 29, 1969, pp. 281ff.; U. Wilckens, 'Die Rechtfertigung Abrahams nach Römer 4', *Studien zur Theologie des alttestamentlichen Überlieferung* (see n. 53), pp. 111ff.; H. Köster, 'Die Auslegung der Abraham-Verheissung in Hebräer 6', ibid., pp. 95ff.) have not praised the *heilsgeschichtlich* line as such, therefore they have not evaluated it as an integral part of his *Theology*. Needless to say, the positions mentioned above have also been criticized.

IV COMPARATIVE ISSUES

1. In order to obtain these statistics it was necessary to compile a complete index for Eichrodt I. Eichrodt has approximately 9,000 references and von Rad 5,000. Citations from the Psalms account for 17% in Eichrodt and 10% in von Rad. Most of the other books are within ½%.

2. For an examination of what he means by this, cf. below, pp. 78ff.

3. This confirms the opinion of those scholars who consider that II is less covenantal than I, since the wisdom material is more general in content and more international in origin.

4. Clearly, this is not the sole reason for his frequent quotation of Deut. 26.

5. Both scholars have a number of ways of referring to the biblical material, i.e., quotations, references within the text of the book, references in footnotes, references in footnotes which follow a 'cf.'. Greater precision would be gained if they were careful to use these different methods to indicate different degrees of proximity between what they say and the biblical material.

6. Von Rad deals with Nazirites and Rechabites only in the 'History of Yahwism'.

7. They are dealt with briefly in the 'History of Yahwism' and in connection with the Hebrew idea of time, but not in P or Deuteronomy.

8. R. E. Clements, 'The Problem of OT Theology', *LQHR* 190, 1965, p. 13.

9. Cf. however, I. 103f., 393; II. 20, 31, 36, 271, 450.

10. Their comments within their *Theologies* have been supplemented by indications given in some of their other works.

11. It is not always necessary to make such decisions before the material can be used, so they may disagree far more than the indications would suggest. These figures include the opinions expressed in their commentaries.

12. Cf. Eichrodt I. 232.

13. Cf. above p. 62.

14. On the whole Eichrodt is critical of anything which is at all systematic within the OT itself (cf. I. 459, II. 440). However he does write as though ideas developed according to some divine necessity (cf. I. 143, 163; II. 383, 500). He uses this presupposition, unconsciously perhaps, to extrapolate lines of development where there is no material evidence and to exclude ideas which are evidenced but which he considers to be alien.

15. Cf. I. G. Barbour, *Issues in Science and Religion*, London 1966, p. 157, for the use of this term.

16. E.g. W. A. Irwin, 'The Study of Israel's Religion', *VT* 7, 1957, pp. 113ff.

17. 'Les Rapports du Nouveau et de l'Ancien Testaments', *Le problème biblique*, ed. J. Boisset, Paris 1955, pp. 105ff.

18. *ZAW* 47, 1929, p. 90.

19. For a survey of contemporary attitudes, cf. F. N. Jaspers, 'The Relation of the OT to the New', *ExpT* LXXVIII, 1967, pp. 228ff., 267ff.

20. *Le problème biblique*, p. 123.

21. Cf. e.g. Amos 5. 18ff.

22. Cf. D. S. Russell, *Method and Message*, pp. 291f.

23. Cf. I. 171, 258, 433, 471; II. 44, 79, 228f., 264f., 348f., 393, 495, 528.

24. Contrast his procedure for demons (II. 227f.) where the development was similar.

25. His earlier theoretical essays also indicate his position, cf. especially

his essay on typology, *OTI*, pp. 17ff.

26. I have restricted my comments to the *most important* of the *central* issues. There are also many minor ambiguities and dubious points. To investigate these important but, from our point of view, peripheral issues, e.g. von Rad's claims about the NT and Qumran and the Rabbinic use of the OT, would require another book.

27. 'Typological Interpretation of the OT', *OTI*, pp. 17ff.; cf. note on p. 17.

28. *OTI*, p. 38; cf. II. 371.

29. *OTI*, pp. 17ff.; cf. II. 364ff.

30. *OTI*, p. 21.

31. *OTI*, p. 37; cf. II. 371f.

32. *OTI*, pp. 28f., 38.

33. *OTI*, pp. 224ff.

34. Cf. below pp. 79f.

35. Cf. below p. 81.

36. *Old and New*, pp. 103ff.

37. N. W. Porteous, 'The Relevance of the OT', in *Living The Mystery*, Oxford 1967, pp. 162f.

38. *OTI*, p. 36.

39. Cf. H. H. Rowley, *The Unity of the Bible*, London 1953, pp. 20, 98.

40. If it is feasible to do this here, why does von Rad make so much fuss about saving history in the main part of his *Theology*? He recognizes a relative independence and validity of ideas which are not specifically part of salvation history.

41. I.e., in contrast to the NT's understanding of the OT.

42. Cf. *OTI*, p. 36.

43. This is omitted from German II[5].

44. This statement presupposes that 'All presentation of history is . . . open to the future' (II. 361) and that therefore no distinction should be made between history and prophecy. We may agree that much of the history was written with a future in view, although this future was often the past from the point of view of the narrator. Anyway, both history and prophecy had a specific idea of the future and the application of these writings to other events, which they did not envisage, would 'do violence' to them. Not every re-actualization can be accepted as legitimate.

45. Cf. e.g. B. Lindars, *NT Apologetic. The Doctrinal Significance of OT Quotations*, London 1961.

46. II. 386.

47. Cf. J. Jeremias, *Jesus' Promise to the Nations*, ET (SBT 24), 1958, esp. pp. 40ff.

48. E.g. Mark 10. 17ff.

49. E.g. Mark 10. 2ff.

50. E.g. Mark 1. 2; Rom. 9–11.

51. Both cases can be paralleled within the OT. Von Rad sees the relation of the OT to the NT as like the story of Jacob at Bethel, where we have only the absorbed story. In fact it is more like the Chronicler's History, where we still have in its original form, in the Deuteronomic History, the material which he used and altered.

52. *TLZ* 68, 1943, cols. 231f.; cf. II. 388f.

53. *OTI*, p. 36.

54. Von Rad tries to make this more plausible by arguing on pp. 333f. that the use of OT *language* in the NT is no different 'in principle' from the use of OT *narratives and predictions*. However, the use of prophetic predictions in relation to Christ, seems to me to raise a different order of questions from the borrowing of terminology.

55. For a brief analysis of this concept, cf. R. Gruner, 'Uniqueness in Nature and History', *Philosophical Quarterly* 19, 1969, pp. 145ff.

56. Eichrodt I. 513f.

57. In a private letter to Dr G. Wenham, von Rad says that he considers it more promising to set OT texts within their OT horizons than within a comparative religion context.

58. Cf. above pp. 44ff.

59 Cf. I. 41ff., 121ff.; see also 'Offenbarung und Geschichte im Alten Testament', *TZ* 4, 1948, pp. 321ff.

60. *History and the Gods,* chs. 1 and 5.

61. Ibid., pp. 95f.

62. S. Mowinckel, 'General Oriental and Specific Israelite Elements in the Israelite Conception of the Sacral Kingdom', *The Sacral Kingship* (Studies in the History of Religion 4), Leiden 1955, p. 288. Cf. R. Benedict, *Patterns of Culture*, London 1935, p. 33.

63. *Patterns of Culture*, p. 164.

64. Cf. Th. C. Vriezen, 'The Study of the OT and the History of Religion' *VTS* 17, 1968, pp. 1ff.

65. Cf. Eichrodt I. 25f.

66. 'Die Aufgabe der alttestamentlicher Forschung', *ZAW* 42, 1924, p. 10.

67. We may see in this attitude a further connection between Eichrodt's *Theology* and neo-orthodoxy.

68. Perhaps Eichrodt hoped to avoid this situation by claiming that Israel's religion was unique in the consistency with which she maintained her beliefs, cf. I. 517.

69. Cf. H. H. Rowley, *The Unity of the Bible*, London 1953, pp. 6f.: 'This interest in OT theology testifies to the growing sense of the unity of the OT', and J. Barr, *The Ecumenical Review* 21, 1969, p. 137: 'The period of "biblical theology" seemed to emphasize the unity of the Bible. . . . More recent scholarship has been occupied with the problem of the diversity of the Bible.'

70. For a summary of the significance of 'unity' for OT Theologies, see F. C. Prussner, 'The Covenant of David and the Problem of Unity in OT Theology', *Transitions in Biblical Scholarship* (Essays in Divinity 6), Chicago 1968, pp. 16ff.

71. Undoubtedly Eichrodt appears to over-systematize, so von Rad's criticism is not without some justification, cf. Eichrodt's comment on 'God's Wrath', 'the real meaning . . . can only be derived from the whole . . .' which applies *mutatis mutandis* to every aspect of Israel's faith. Further evidence for this is his stress that ideas developed necessarily in a particular direction.

This is no mere logical necessity but the consequence of the divine pressure upon Israel's beliefs.

72. Cf. E. Jacob, *Theology of the OT*, ET London 1958, pp.12.

73. Cf. above pp.68ff.

74. In order to include the Bible as a whole, Eichrodt only has to extend this principle.

75. Obviously the problem of 'selection' rears its ugly head at this point. Eichrodt tries to use the 'selection' provided by the OT itself; this is another reason why he chooses covenant. His critics see in this choice his own, rather than the OT's, selection.

76. What this might be I do not know, not even that they were all expressed in Hebrew!

77. W. Zimmerli has tried to work out the significance of this for the task of OT Theology: cf. 'Alttestamentliche Traditionsgeschichte und Theologie', *Probleme biblischer Theologie*, ed. H. W. Wolff, München 1971, pp.632ff.; cf. also R. Smend, *Die Mitte des Alten Testaments* (ThSt 101), 1970.

78. Von Rad's *Wisdom in Israel*, is really an attempt to show that and how the wisdom material must also be integrated with Yahwism if it is to be understood properly.

79. Cf. H. H. Rowley, 'The Unity of the OT', *BJRL* 29, 1945, pp.326ff.; cf. D. N. Freedman, 'The Law and the Prophets', *VTS* 9, 1962, pp.250ff.; R. E. Clements, *Prophecy*, pp.126ff.

80. Even this may not be impossible, cf. S. V. McCasland, 'A comment on Dr Wright's paper', *JBR* 20, 1952, p.200.

81. G. Fohrer, 'Remarks on the Modern Interpretation of the Prophets', *JBL* 80, 1961, p.314.

82. R. J. Thompson, *Moses and the Law in a Century of Criticism since Graf*, *VTS* 19, 1970, p.171.

83. G. E. Wright, 'Wherein lies the Unity of the Bible', *JBR* 20, 1952, p.201; cf. also, 'The Unity of the Bible', *SJT* 8, 1955, pp.337ff.

84. Cf. R. C. Dentan, 'The Nature and Function of OT Theology', *JBR* 14, 1946, p.21, 'If one will approach OT religion looking . . . for the organic unity which underlies it . . . he will find that out of the multiplicity of phenomena a pattern will gradually emerge . . . which includes prophet and priest and wise man and the humble devotee at the shrine.'

85. Cf. above pp.60ff.

86. For brief comments on its importance for a wider range of OT Theologies, cf. R. Rendtorff, 'The Concept of Revelation in Ancient Israel', *Revelation as History*, ed. W. Pannenberg, ET London 1969, pp.25ff. The OT's understanding of revelation was the subject of a discussion between Rendtorff and Zimmerli, cf. *EvTh* 22, 1962, pp.15ff. and 621ff. A brief account had been given earlier by H. Haag, '"Offenbaren" in der hebräischen Bibel', *TZ* 16, 1960, pp.251ff.; cf. also, R. Knierim, 'Offenbarung im Alten Testament', *Probleme biblischer Theologie*, pp.206ff. The viability and applicability of 'revelation' to the biblical tradition has been investigated by G. Downing, *Has Christianity a Revelation?*, London 1964; cf. J. Barr, *Old and New*, pp.82ff. Eichrodt's views can be found in, 'Offenbarung und Geschichte im Alten Testament', *TZ* 4, 1948, pp.321ff.

87. 'Timeless truths' could be truths which have always been known, or truths which are always valid, although not always known by man. This second class need not conflict with 'historical revelation'.

88. Cf. *TZ* 4, 1948, p. 332: 'Here [sc. 'in the events of Moses' time'] one learnt to understand God's essence from history and to describe his activity in the form of history.'

89. Cf. ibid., pp. 326f., where he claims history cannot be understood as acts of God by normal faculties, but only when God announces his will in law or prophecy.

90. Ibid. p. 321: God 'cannot be reached, in any way, by human thought'.

91. Cf. R. Rendtorff, *TLZ* 88, 1963, col. 746ff.; K. Koch, *KuD* 8, 1962, pp. 100ff.; J. Barr, *Old and New*, pp. 98f.

92. There are over ninety occurrences.

93. The only possible exception I have noted is I. 433: 'It would be completely wrong to assume . . .'

94. Cf. above p. 92.

95. The discrepancy could be resolved if what was difficult for us to conceive were the mode and not the clarity of revelation.

96. Cf. the quotation from K. Barth, II. 382.

97. For further criticisms of his concept of revelation cf. F. Baumgärtel (*TLZ* 86, 1961, cols. 895ff.) who criticizes him for ignoring the illumination of people by God and therefore for excluding these 'inner events' from the *Heilsgeschichte*. In contrast to Eichrodt von Rad mentions 'experiences of God' infrequently. Cf. also, J. van der Ploeg, 'Une "Theologie de l'Ancien Testament" est-elle possible?', *Ephemerides Theologicae Lovanienses*, 38, 1962, pp. 431ff.

INDEX OF AUTHORS

INDEX OF SUBJECTS